# Take your learning further with this book's online course.

All the titles in Kogan Page's Creating Success series have individual *CPD-accredited* online courses to help you develop your business and workplace skills.

**Quick and easy-to-use**: 1-hour courses to develop your skills quickly

**CPD accreditation**: Each course awards CPD points and certification for tangible proof of your achievement

**Additional resources**: Downloadable resources will reinforce what you learn

**Bespoke packages**: Discounted corporate and bespoke offers are also available

**Free preview**: Module preview to confirm you are picking the right one

Find out more about the course for this book at
**koganpageonline.com**

D0165539

**Save 25%**
on all courses using the code CREATINGSUCCESS

# CREATING SUCCESS
## SERIES

*Dealing with Difficult People* Roy Lilley

*Decision Making and Problem Solving* John Adair

*Develop Your Leadership Skills* John Adair

*Develop Your Presentation Skills* Theo Theobald

*How to Manage People* Michael Armstrong

*How to Manage Projects* Paul J Fielding

*How to Organize Yourself* John Caunt

*How to Write a Business Plan* Brian Finch

*How to Write a Marketing Plan* John Westwood

*How to Write Reports and Proposals* Patrick Forsyth

*Improve Your Communication Skills* Alan Barker

*Successful Time Management* Patrick Forsyth

*Taking Minutes of Meetings* Joanna Gutmann

The above titles are available from all good bookshops.

For further information on these and other Kogan Page titles, or to order online, visit **www.koganpage.com**.

# How to Manage Projects

Essential project management
skills to deliver on-time,
on-budget results

*Paul J Fielding*

**Publisher's note**

Every possible effort has been made to ensure that the information contained in this book is accurate at the time of going to press, and the publishers and authors cannot accept responsibility for any errors or omissions, however caused. No responsibility for loss or damage occasioned to any person acting, or refraining from action, as a result of the material in this publication can be accepted by the editor, the publisher or the author.

First published in Great Britain and the United States in 2019 by Kogan Page Limited

Apart from any fair dealing for the purposes of research or private study, or criticism or review, as permitted under the Copyright, Designs and Patents Act 1988, this publication may only be reproduced, stored or transmitted, in any form or by any means, with the prior permission in writing of the publishers, or in the case of reprographic reproduction in accordance with the terms and licences issued by the CLA. Enquiries concerning reproduction outside these terms should be sent to the publishers at the undermentioned addresses:

2nd Floor, 45 Gee Street
London
EC1V 3RS
United Kingdom
**www.koganpage.com**

122 W 27th St, 10th Floor
New York, NY 10001
USA

4737/23 Ansari Road
Daryaganj
New Delhi 110002
India

© Paul J Fielding, 2019

The right of Paul J Fielding to be identified as the author of this work has been asserted by him in accordance with the Copyright, Designs and Patents Act 1988.

**ISBNs**

Hardback    978 0 7494 9894 8
Paperback   978 0 7494 8869 7
Ebook       978 0 7494 8902 1

**British Library Cataloguing-in-Publication Data**

A CIP record for this book is available from the British Library.

**Library of Congress Cataloging-in-Publication Control Number**

Names: Fielding, Paul J., author.
Title: How to manage projects : essential project management skills to
    deliver on-time, on-budget results / Paul J. Fielding.
Description: London ; New York : Kogan Page, [2019] | Series: Creating
    success.
Identifiers: LCCN 2019005206 (print) | LCCN 2019008787 (ebook) | ISBN
    9780749489021 (Ebook) | ISBN 9780749488697 (pbk.) | ISBN 9780749498948
    (hardback)
Subjects: LCSH: Project management.
Classification: LCC HD69.P75 (ebook) | LCC HD69.P75 F5425 2019 (print) | DDC
    658.4/04—dc23
LC record available at https://lccn.loc.gov/2019005206

Typeset by Hong Kong FIVE Workshop
Print production managed by Jellyfish
Printed and bound by CPI Group (UK) Ltd, Croydon CR0 4YY

# CONTENTS

# ABOUT THE AUTHOR

Paul J Fielding PhD is a business consultant specializing in developing project management systems, business operations and quality systems for his clients. He has received international awards and recognition (including the Deming Award). He has worked across many industries, technologies and cultures, from large institutions to startups and nonprofits, and has developed a worldwide reputation for developing quality project management systems, international business operations, creating game-changing process innovations, and quality improvement processes. He currently offices out of Portland (Maine), Dallas and New York City.

# ACKNOWLEDGEMENTS

This work would have been impossible without the support and vision from the good people at Kogan Page.

Rebecca Bush has got to be the best editor ever. I love 'war stories', anecdotes, analogies, developing discussions, digging into theory, history and a good joke. These things might be helpful and interesting to some and can play well during presentations (where one customizes material to fit the room). Such things do not always work well in book form. Plus, this book is supposed to help all readers develop a foundation on which you can build your stories, experiences and successes. There are insufficient words (and she'd probably edit them out) to express my appreciation for Rebecca's patience, perceptive eye, sharp knife and skill as an editor (albeit painful at times). She has made this a much better product for you. But if you're ever keen to hear the rest of the story...

Martin Vonderheiden is an excellent project manager, scholar and trainer in his own right. His encouragement got this ball rolling.

John Murphy's friendship brought together key elements that made this happen.

Lastly, and most importantly, God's gift of my loving wife Chian (Tuzy-Tuzi), without whose support, understanding, patience, encouragement, tolerance... well, there is no end of adjectives to describe her importance to making this possible, so I will just leave it at that.

Thank you to all mentioned above, and those not mentioned, who made all this and so much more possible.

# 01

# Project success is more than just one thing

'If we were to do just one thing (or a few things) from this plan you have shown us, which ones would give us success?' After almost any presentation, outlining how a complex problem can be resolved to success, someone inevitably, predictably, tries to appear smart, crafty or shrewd by asking that question, or something similar. It seems to be human nature to look for the one thing, or just a few things, the simple things, that if we just did that, if we followed that recipe, success would be ours!

When asked this question, I take off my wristwatch, or bring out my pocket watch, and slide it across the table. I collect old-fashioned, mechanical skeleton watches. When looking at these watches, you can see all the gears, the oscillating balance wheel, the escapement mechanism, the mainspring, and more, all working together to mark off the moments of our lives. To me, these devices are functional pieces of art in action.

As I push my watch across the table, I ask the parsimonious person, 'Which few gears, if you just had them, would compute the time for you?' Clearly, the question is absurd. Computing the time is beyond the unaided abilities of any singular component of any watch. All the parts must function together, playing their role, aiding each other, to meet the requirement of telling us the time.

The same is true of successful projects. Successful projects are beyond the unaided abilities of any single person. Many things must function together, playing their role, to meet the requirements of the project. Successful projects are a bit like building a custom-crafted watch; there are principles, skills, experiences, knowledge, tools, and much more which the project manager (watchmaker) must apply. But because it's a *custom* watch, there is no 'recipe' to follow. The project manager (watchmaker) must *craft* the solution to answer the challenge. This book will help you develop your knowledge, perspective, principles and insights on what it takes to answer the complex challenge of creating a successful project.

# How to use this book

We will start with a practical look at some fundamentals of project management and explore the implications that develop from there. We will define what makes an effort rise to the level of being a project. Once we define something as a project, what are some implications that follow? We will look at different types of project models, issues with quality planning, staffing, cost and project schedule management (project time management), and much more. This text is not designed as a replacement for a particular project management qualification or methodology, but as a practical primer to help you manage projects you are facing.

If you don't know one end of a project from another and you've picked this up out of interest, to see whether project management could be for you – welcome! I recommend starting at the beginning, and reading through the chapters in order. Build your foundations of project management thinking and philosophy. Then read it all again, and develop some experiences by applying what you've learnt on small-scale projects first, giving special attention to the final chapter. Build on those experiences to make each new project better than the last!

If you've had projects dropped in your lap and are feeling out of your depth – welcome! You are not alone. This book is designed to be *practical*, with useful guidance. You may want to flip to the chapter on the topic that is giving you particular stress, for a bit of firefighting. In projects, rarely is a problem just about one thing. Many things can influence an issue. So, I'd still recommend taking time to flip through the rest of the book to shore up your overall practices and perspectives.

If you're an experienced project manager already – welcome! You're probably someone who's always developing their skills and improving your craft. You may be looking for insights that go beyond administrative tools or the latest fad. This book is written from the perspective of applied principles that you might find timeless. Hopefully, they can help guide your effectiveness regardless of what specific tools you might be using. You may have figured much of this out already – but maybe you'll find some things you hadn't considered, or maybe the framework will give you a structure on which you can build, refine and improve your thinking and future projects.

Whatever your starting point, the following chapters have been written to help you develop a better, practical understanding of this field. There is no one thing, or even a few things, that make complex projects successful. Here you will find some of the many topics and core principles that, as a successful project manager, you will consider, balance and craft into effective solutions that will make your projects successful.

## 02

# The accidental project manager

## What is this going to take?

**The scenario**: Around the meeting room sit colleagues who are important to your working life. You have voiced some good ideas. They like your thoughts. All agree on the general course of action. People think to themselves that the desired goal is clear. How we are going to get there is not so clear.

The leader looks you square in the eye and says, 'This project is important. I think you have a handle on the key ideas. I want you to manage this to success.' The leader looks at your colleagues. 'We all agreed on this?' Silence follows. 'Great!' Looking right at you, 'We have our project manager! Do we have anything else to cover?' There is a short pause. 'Great; we're done.' The leader, while quickly packing their things, says, 'I have to catch a plane. See you all in two weeks.' The leader turns to you with a big smile. 'This is a real opportunity. Go forth and be successful, and we all win big. Mess this up… well, we don't need to talk about that right now.' There are too many thoughts running through your head to say anything. People who you wanted to catch are now walking out the door. As the leader follows the others to the door, they look over their shoulder and say to you, 'When I get back, I want to see some plans from you on what it will take to make this happen, on time and on budget! See you then. Enjoy!' With that, they are gone.

Does the above scenario feel familiar? Often, without planning to be a project manager, many people find themselves having to manage a project. They 'accidentally' (if you will) ended up in the role of project manager. Their part in the project can become an accident waiting to happen. How can one avoid such misery? How can one manage a project to success?

The chapters that follow will give you some tools that will help you to address the above questions. A theme throughout this text is that we can only give you philosophies, concepts, ideas and methods that may be helpful; there is no recipe that will guarantee success. You will have to figure out how to custom craft the application of this material to your situation. Project management is a job of taking skills, tools, information, knowledge, experience, and I dare say wisdom, to make order and solutions out of challenges and problems.

Let's begin by asking:

1  What is a project?
2  What is a project manager?

# What is a project?

For our practical purpose, when we talk about a project, what do we mean? Dictionary definitions are great for those who study the language. Academic definitions are wonderful for those who wish to analyse nuances or conduct research. For our purposes, we need to understand the common, colloquial, business context in which you will find this term used.

To determine if an effort rises to the level of being a project, and thus should have a project manager, I consider seven characteristics of the effort. Okay, there are really eight characteristics, but the first one is so basic that I am counting that as number zero: all projects are temporary efforts. Yet, being a temporary effort, by itself, it does not make the effort a project; but if the effort is not temporary (eg, if it is ongoing maintenance, operations, etc) then it needs a different type of oversight. With that in mind, Table 2.1 is a decision table one can use to test the characteristics of an effort, to see if that effort is a project, or something else. Take this moment to review Table 2.1.

A theme of Table 2.1 is that something rises to the level of being a project when, considering each characteristic of the effort, the average unaided abilities of a person are not easily able to resolve that characteristic. Or, if when considering the *aggregate* of all the characteristics, the same is true. This feature of a project, that managing the activity requires more than the unaided abilities of the average person, is important. Once we recognize that feature, then by default we acknowledge several things. First, you are going to need some tools, methods, practices, assistance... you are going to need something to supplement your abilities, if you are to be successful. In the subsequent chapters, we develop principles that guide the use of tools, methods and approaches that help project managers go beyond their unaided abilities.

Our definition of a project also means that if you have something that measures up to the level of being a project, then that effort *needs* a project manager. One classic error organizations can make is to let an activity develop into being a project without recognizing it as such, and without formally empowering someone to manage that effort. With little thought, I bet you can see how this might happen. Things start out small. Someone thinks the lead person 'should' be able to just lead or manage all this. As things grow, as we get into the effort, we find out... it is a project; it takes more to manage than those in charge anticipated. This effort is something that requires the aid of tools, resources, special techniques, teams, and so on. The person leading the effort realizes that this is going to take more than their singular, unaided abilities to make this a success. They are accidentally managing a project. If the effort continues without recognizing they are a project manager, and that the situation needs proper management beyond just 'doing it on the fly', then something like chaos, kerfuffles and problems seem to be the inevitable result.

**Table 2.1** Characteristics that make an effort a project

| Feature to consider | Logical test | |
|---|---|---|
| 0. Is this a temporary or transient effort? | **NO**<br>This effort is not temporary or transient. It is permanent, perpetual or enduring (eg, maintenance efforts, operations efforts, etc). Then this effort is not a project. It is something else. | **YES**<br>This effort is temporary or transient. The effort may be a project, depending on features 1–7. Continue. |
| | **Can the average person manage this feature without aids?** | |
| 1. The requirements that define or specify the goal | YES<br>Then continue | NO<br>Then this effort is a project! |
| 2. Orchestrating the steps over the time required | YES<br>Then continue | NO<br>Then this effort is a project! |
| 3. Coordinating the resources (people, supplies, facilities, logistics) | YES<br>Then continue | NO<br>Then this effort is a project! |

4. Assuring compliance with standards, regulations, regulators, evaluation criteria

YES
Then continue

NO
Then this effort is a project!

5. Establishing the creation, manufacture, delivery or installation

YES
Then continue

NO
Then this effort is a project!

6. Cross-organizational or group dynamics

YES
Then continue

NO
Then this effort is a project!

7. If 1–6 above were all YES, consider the combination of them all taken together.

YES
Then this is not a project. It may be a significant effort, but we will not call this effort a project.

NO
Then this effort is a project!

If you answered NO to any of 1–7 (and YES to 0) then we will call this effort a project.

## A short, practical definition of what is a project manager: superhero!

A successful project manager will often appear to be on the level of a real-life superhero (at least in my book!). Like Superman's Clark Kent, project managers may have this mild-mannered persona. In one aspect of their role, they just collect the data, develop plans and track activities, studying the impacts of change requests and such. Like Clark Kent, they may appear to be just that mild-mannered reporter of the daily project news.

Then something happens and trouble comes to the city of Metropolis that is your project; like Superman, the project manager comes to the rescue. From their perspective, they see innovative connections between various activities – and before you know it, they are able to plan around the problem (ideally with a single bound). As they conduct the requirements review, they spot open-ended scope definitions, firm up weak acceptance criteria and discover issues the team must fix (almost as if they were viewing the requirements with x-ray vision). As they schedule all the activities and interactions, and mobilize the organization's efforts, the power of a smoothly functioning team is awesome (almost like the power of a speeding locomotive). By the way: in case it is not obvious, the project manager is the person who is responsible for orchestrating and managing all the components we listed above, leading to the successful outcome of that effort. Indeed, when considering all these things a project manager must do (and the many other things we will detail throughout the rest of this book), the importance to an organization of a successful project manager can seem similar to that of a superhero.

## Self-inventory: Do I have what it takes to be a project manager?

Being a successful project manager also depends on your personality. That is to say, as a project manager, much of your success depends on how you think about problems, how you frame your approach to addressing issues, and how you relate to people. Those soft skills, those 'human engineering' skills, they too make a huge difference to a project manager's success. Much of project management 'science' spends time on technical things a project manager must do, such as: vetting requirements, developing activity plans, status reporting, and so on. Behind all those processes, plans and reports, there are people. In any project, people are central to achieving the sought-after goal. Anytime someone needs people for success, the so-called soft skills of human engineering become critical to success. A project manager's personality, the attitude they bring to the interactions, the way they approach and manage things at a human level, are important, even critical, to the success of the project.

Return to our opening scenario. Imagine that after that event, you and I meet for a chat; maybe over coffee or dinner – just to chat, as friends. You relate to me that you are happy about this opportunity. Yet you feel that you are just a little in over your head. This is a high-profile deal. You wonder aloud to me if you have what it takes to make this work. With that perspective, I encourage us to explore for a moment what tends to be the personality of a successful project manager.

Yes, you are good at organizing things. You can find the important details in the big picture, and you can build the big picture from the details. You are a good communicator. You can listen to others, synthesize their thoughts into concise headlines, and often you are able to express their ideas better than they can. When you have a point to make, you express your ideas in a way so people get it! You are creative at finding solutions, where others are stuck. And, of course, you and I are chatting because you are a person with good emotional intelligence and organizational intelligence. You know when people are stressing, and how to work with them while they are stressing. Plus, you know how to pull the right people together to get a job done. You are what some people might call a high self-monitor (you understand how individuals and groups perceive your actions, and as a result people perceive you well; they trust you). When your friends get into an argument, you are the one that they both turn to for understanding – and you always seem to get them back together. You are not afraid of conflict; to you, conflict is just another thing to manage. When it comes to change, it does not rock you back on your heels. Actually, you see change as a process. You are often the one that drives change, because to you that change is something we all desire. To get to the goal, we have to go down this path, and you can negotiate that path to get us there.

Yet, despite all these things above, you wonder, do you have what it takes to be a good project manager? You look at people who have mastered that new tool from that specialty software house. Or how about people who took that course in that method everyone has been talking about? You are not a professional project manager and you know it. You wonder what are the first things you need to think about, if you are going to be a good project manager, for this project?

The first thing I am going to tell you is despite all the fancy tools, terms and techniques professional project managers and textbooks may throw around, the success or failure of a project manager tends to hinge on their effectiveness at working with people. A project manager's overall emotional intelligence is important to success. In 1936, in Dale Carnegie's iconic text *How To Win Friends and Influence People* he points out that '... about 15 percent of one's financial success is due to one's technical knowledge and about 85 percent is due to skill in human engineering – to personality and the ability to lead people' (Carnegie, 1981). Over the years, others have studied this claim. Despite minor variations in the statistics between studies, they all point to the same general idea: emotional intelligence – how you work with others – accounts for success more than technical skills. Yes, technical skills are important. They are necessary! Success cannot happen without them. Nevertheless, to some degree, technical skills in a field are something of a commodity. Yes, some people have better technical skills, and that certainly helps them in their job. Still, once an adequate level of technical competency is brought to bear on the problem, the soft skills become the critical differentiator.

The field of project management, in the past, emphasized tools, techniques and systems. More recently, studies have begun to show that the 'soft skills' may have more impact on project success than many previously realized (Creasy and Anantatmula, 2013). Table 2.2 is a checklist of soft skills that I find are important to being a successful project manager.

**Table 2.2**  Characteristics that make an effort a project

| Characteristic | Yes<br>Neutral<br>No |
| --- | --- |

**Are they organized?[1]**
- Is their approach to things organized?
- Do they conduct themselves in an organized way?
- Are they effective at the way they organize things? That is, their efforts at organizing helps move things forward – it does not paralyse things.

**Are they a good communicator?**
- Are they a good listener – can they effectively express back to the speaker or others what someone said?
- Can they effectively interpret and process other forms of communication, including visual and written?
- Can they distil the important points from what they have heard or read?
- Can they make an effective and compelling point to their audience?

**Are they innovative?**
- Does this person show an ability to find creative solutions?
- Do they have 'puzzle-solving' skills?

**Can they effectively self-monitor?**
- Do they understand how individuals and groups perceive their actions?
- Is this person someone people are likely to trust?

**Do they have good character?**
- Is this person trustworthy?
- Can they maintain confidences?[2]
- Do they rarely tend to speak badly of others?[3]

**Table 2.2**   *continued*

| Characteristic | Yes Neutral No |
|---|---|
| | |

**Can they manage conflict?**
- Have they demonstrated an ability to resolve and negotiate conflicts?
- Can they see multiple views of the same issue?
- Do they tend to resort to compromise, or can they synergize?[4]

**Can they manage change?**
- Do they embrace new things?
- Are they able to develop processes for addressing a never before seen problem?[5]

**Are they a people person?**
- Do they like working with people?
- Do they seem to make connections easily with others?
- Are they a positive person?
- Do they help others around them to be happy?

**Can they make good decisions?**
- Do they try to get all the facts before making a decision?
- Can they make decisions in a specific time frame? Including if that means a decision must be made without all the information?

**Do they have personal balance?**
- Are they able to show a balance between conflicting demands:
    - in a business setting?
    - in a personal setting?
    - between work and personal demands?

**NOTES**

1 Some people consider being organized as a technical skill. I understand that point, but I tend to feel that being organized is also a mindset that fits with the soft skills – so I am including it here.

2 PMs will be exposed to much sensitive information. They must be able to keep it confidential.

3 I find that people who speak badly of others tend to make for bad PMs because they can always find others to blame. Successful PMs find and successfully use strengths.

4 Compromise is a bad thing, because it means everyone is a bit unhappy. Synergizing is the 'third' option that makes everyone happy.

5 Giving someone an unsolvable problem to address, and watching how they approach it, I feel gives me much insight about how they might handle problems during the course of a project. But that is just one thought.

Is this table exhaustive and complete? No! Are there things there that you might change? Hang on to that thought! Here is the problem with writing a book: I put something down and it becomes static. If we were meeting face-to-face, or brainstorming this issue with your colleagues, we would develop a list that your team knows summarizes the human-engineering skills that are important to being successful in your organization. Many of these things are common across all types of organization, and it is good to have a starting point. But what works in your organization might be unique. In Chapter 3 we develop the importance of being sensitive to organizational context. Consider this checklist, and things here, as starting places. Then build on them.

The key point here is that if you more or less have these traits, if you are generally skilled at the art of human engineering, then most likely you can sort through the rest. Technology comes and goes. The human condition, the skills that involve the management of people, from what I can tell, does not seem to have changed much over the millennia. Therefore, if someone asked me to interview candidates for the job of project manager, I would first look for indications that the person had these soft skills – probably using something similar to the checklist above. If their attitude and people skills fit the job, fit the organization and fit the challenge that is before them, then in my experience they can sort the other technology details and acquire that knowledge as needed along the way.

## Summary points

- Many people find themselves accidentally managing a project. Either they fell into the position, or the effort grew into a project. If you find yourself managing a project, it is important to have that recognized so that the appropriate level of focus and resources can be brought to bear on the effort so that it will be successful.

- Our definition of a project is an effort that is both temporary in nature, and yet sufficiently difficult or complex so that the average person would not be able to successfully manage all the components of the effort without the aid of tools, or other means of assistance.

- A successful project manager will be someone who can manage the technical aspects of all the things that must come together to make this effort a success, and also has the right personal skills, attitude, approach and balance towards managing the components of the project.

- Lastly, projects are performed by people. A successful project manager will have strong human-engineering skills for managing the people dynamics that are inherently part of every project.

## References

Carnegie, D (1981) *How to Win Friends and Influence People: Revised edition*, Vermilion, London, xiv

Creasy, T and Anantatmula, V S (2013) From every direction: how personality traits and dimensions of project managers can conceptually affect project success, *Project Management Journal*, **44** (6), 36–51

## 03

# Where does a project manager fit in the organization?

## The role of the PMO

One measure of a successful project manager will come from how well you function within your organization. Successfully driving tasks to closure will not be enough. By definition, a project is going to take more than your unaided abilities. You will have to leverage the organization about you. A good way to find out how your position fits into your organization will be to enlist the aid of your local Project Management Office (PMO).

### What's in a name?

Across businesses, the same things can be called by different names. I have seen PMOs called Project Performance Offices (PPOs), Project Centers of Excellence (PCOEs), the Project Support Office (PSO). Someone reading this book will be working in an environment where the function of a PMO has a name I never imagined. Once I consulted at a company (which had nothing to do with the aerospace industry) that called their project management office 'The Tower/Air Traffic Control'. They called the project managers 'pilots' and they called projects 'flights'. They had developed their own jargon around this concept.

Your organization may have a different name for the functions in this chapter. Be sensitive to that. The language we are using is the industry standard nomenclature that certified project managers will use. If you want to look up more about this subject, you should be able to find it by using the terms we use here.

If you are working in an organization of significant size, you might find they have established a PMO. If so, it is important that you connect your project to that PMO. If your organization does not have a PMO, then you will need to address many things on your own. For the moment, let us consider the situation where your organization has a PMO.

## If a PMO exists

While every PMO is different, in general the PMO is responsible for:

- defining processes;
- setting policies; and
- outlining procedures.

They most likely also include:

- required governance controls;
- standard tools your organization uses;
- information reporting methods;
- templates, checklists, etc.

More thorough PMOs will even have databases of past projects, a library of standard planning times for activities, and so on.

Whatever they can provide to you – *use it*! While there are similarities between all organizations, each organization has its unique issues that you will need to manage. Your PMO will have already seen many of these situations. Your project will have a better chance of succeeding by making use of insights the PMO can provide. Build on the lessons learnt from the experiences of others. By doing so, your management of your project will be that much smarter, and that much more likely to succeed.

In general, people talk about three different types of PMO: supportive, controlling and directive. The discussion here outlines idealized concepts. Probably no organization implements any of these PMOs exactly as described; this is just a framework to facilitate your thinking about PMOs. Connect with the PMO of your organization to find out exactly how they work.

## Supportive PMO

A supportive PMO does just that and only that. They give you support in the form of templates, guidelines, access to libraries, information, training, and generally whatever others may have filed with them. They might have people who will consult with you as you start your project, but they are only there to give you input on what they think might be helpful. They are not going to control your project or be responsible for anything about your project. If your industry must comply with codes, regulations, ordinances or laws, a supportive PMO will most likely have that information handy.

Additionally, a supportive PMO might serve as a repository for past projects. Yes, your project is unique. Yet components of other previous projects might be similar. How did others approach similar issues? Can you apply their successes to your project? If so, copy it! If you were thinking of approaching something in a particular way, and you see that a previous person did something similar and their approach led to failure – try a different approach.

The supportive PMO is not there to control you. They are just there to give you some support. In this type of PMO environment, you get to do whatever you want with your project.

---

**Example**

Planning a business trip to meet a prospective client

Imagine your project was to plan a business trip to meet with a prospective client. A supportive PMO would be a bit like that good friend who has helpful advice handy for you to leverage. They might know who had been out to that client or customer before, or who had visited similar clients. They will let you know if there are special things you need to consider about this trip (eg, will you need a passport, visa, vaccinations). Maybe they know of some corporate deals on rental cars and airline tickets. They might share with you forms you can use for submitting your expense report. Maybe they will have a suggested form for how you might log and report on this contact. And they might have some sample contracts that you can use as a template for sealing the deal with the client. But in the end, how you get there, what you do on the trip, how you write up your contact and report on it, and what terms you strike for the deal with this client – it is all up to you. They are there simply to support you in your efforts. Take their advice, or don't. It's no sweat off their back! Hopefully, you find them helpful.

---

## Controlling PMO

A controlling PMO controls what you *shall* do for your project. They may provide everything a supportive PMO provides, but they do not stop there. If your industry has standards, rules, regulations, codes, laws, or the like, with which you must comply, then this type of PMO typically provides you with a list of those things. You may have to show the people running this type of PMO that your project complied with these requirements. If so, they will most likely provide you with the forms, processes or methods for delivering that information to them. They will also specify for you things such as:

- what tools to use;
- what methodologies to use;
- what templates to use;
- software, libraries, and so on, to use;
- meeting requirements;
- reporting requirements;
- governance frameworks you must implement;
- and all sorts of other things.

While a controlling PMO controls what you shall do for your project (and they may have some 'shall nots' – for example, maybe they will say 'you shall not contact vendors directly – all vendor contact must go through procurement' and things like that), they typically do not get into the specifics of what you do to manage your project. They control the form; framework; style; format; process; governance structure you must set up; reporting; and all the things by which you will manage your project. But what actually gets done in the project, how your project works, and the responsibility for executing and delivering the project – that's all yours!

---

### Example
Planning a business trip to meet a prospective client

Think about your business trip again. Imagine modelling customer contact after a controlling PMO. We will call them the Controlling Customer Engagement Department (CCED). They will tell you which expense reporting tools to use, which airlines and rental car companies to use. They'll tell you what things you're not allowed to do on the trip ('This company will not reimburse you for alcoholic drinks consumed on the trip'). Still, it is up to you to book your own plane tickets, make your own rental car reservations and measure the success or failure of the trip itself.

If you ignore the CCED and book your plane tickets on an unapproved airline, complications might follow. You might not be reimbursed for the tickets. The 'Big Boss' might need to approve your deviation from policy. If you modify contract templates beyond simply filling in the blanks, a troublesome review by the legal department may be in your future. So while you control *what* you do, they control *how* you do it.

## Directive PMO

A directive PMO is often an independent organization within the corporate structure. A team of project managers report to an executive who is on the same level as the other department heads. When a department starts a project, a project manager from the directive PMO takes on the project as a full manager. Organizationally, they have the rank of manager, and they take control of the project.

This structure has several benefits. It assures that:

- a common methodology gets used and perfected over time;
- a standard terminology and language develops throughout the organization;
- repeatable, predictable processes are used;
- common tools are used.

While the importance to an organization of these things cannot be overstated, the project manager also has some independence from the organizational management that is sponsoring the project. There is a 'dark side' of management, which no one likes to discuss. Imagine being a direct report to Darth Vader. Imagine expressing a lack of faith in his plans to him, or maybe you have bad news that his latest plan is flawed, overly ambitious, or is about to fall apart. I'm sure we can all guess how that situation would turn out! Hopefully, your line manager is not Darth Vader. Yet, we humans can all unintentionally have a little bit of the 'dark side' within us. Having the PM report to a different organization buffers dark-side tendencies that might inappropriately influence a project manager. Specifically:

1 The project manager (PM) can operate without fear of direct retaliation for delivering bad news.

2 It becomes a bit more difficult for the line manager (LM) to attempt a coup/undermine the PM's authority. An LM attempting such a thing would have to contend with peers running the directive PMO.

3 In strong directive PMOs, the PM will even participate in the performance review of the assigned human resources. This helps establish the authority of the PM on the project.

Of course, LMs might not like these checks and balances. They might believe projects could get done quicker if they had more direct control. While this model has its fans, it also has its detractors.

## Example

Planning a business trip to meet a prospective client

Think about your business trip again. Imagine modelling customer contact after a directive PMO – ponder a Directive Customer Engagement Department (DCED). When the *potential* client becomes an *actual* client, your department will be responsible for implementing the solution for most aspects of the ongoing relationship. However, under this model, you will not visit that potential client by yourself, or engage in any negotiations with them by yourself. The DCED would manage that contact. They would be responsible for booking the plane tickets, making the hotel reservations, ensuring the appropriate people from the legal department are included, the appropriate people in management have bought into this pursuit, and so on. Your team will still be responsible for the technical content of the meeting, many of the things discussed in the meeting, and delivering the product should your company land this client. But the DCED will manage the contact, the negotiations, the recording and reporting of that contact. In many organizations, this model might sound absurd. Yet, some organizations implement models similar to this. Specifically, some companies do things like this to avoid litigious problems, prevent high-value misunderstandings, maintain security or address sensitive issues.

There are many more pros and cons to each of these models. There are some other models not mentioned here. Each organization designs their own PMO model, which may be a blend of several different models and philosophies. You need to find out if your organization has a PMO, regardless of the type. If it does, get plugged in.

# What if a PMO does not exist?

If a PMO does not exist in your organization, you will still need to address the things that it might have done for you. A PMO would have defined your role as a project manager within the organization. All projects exist within an organizational context. How you and your project function in that context is just as important as driving tasks to closure.

Organizational context questions that a PMO would have handled, which you must do for yourself, include things such as:

- What has previously *not* worked in your organization?
- What works well in your organization?

- What organizational policies and procedures will be relevant to your project?

- How will you interface with the organization about you, and how will they interface with you?

- How will you relate to the management team around you?

- How will your authority be established and maintained (and what authority do you *not* have)?

When (not if, but when) project issues develop, how will you and your management team address them? In our discussion for the directive PMO, we alluded to the idea that bringing disappointing news to your direct management team might have unhealthy outcomes for your career. There will be disappointing moments in every project. How will the organization support you during those moments?

Take some time to revisit our opening scenario. There, the leader said, 'This is a real opportunity. Go forth and be successful, and we all win big. Mess this up… well, we don't need to talk about that right now.' But you *are* going to need to talk about that – maybe right now. Even if you do everything right, it is almost certain there will be disappointing moments in the life of any project. Who is going to be your angel protector? Who will be your firewall? What is the plan for your career post project, assuming not everything goes perfectly (through no fault of your own)?

Along with figuring out the organizational dynamics, you also need to figure out the infrastructure for your project. What tools will you use? There are many good tools out there. This book will not recommend one over the other. There is a good reason for that: what makes projects succeed is the application of the timeless principles of project management. Once you understand these principles, then you can use almost any 'good' tool to fill the needs. Yes, some tools are better than other tools. Some tools will help you make better use of your time. But tools will change; technology is ephemeral. The basics of what makes a project manager successful are slow to change, and may even be timeless.

With all that said, you still have to decide on what tools you are going to use for the environment in which you will be working. Without a PMO, that choice may be entirely up to you, or other forces or traditions within your organization may influence that choice. Start by checking with your colleagues in your organization. Being compatible with, and playing well with, others (so to speak) is an important organizational dynamic that helps one be successful.

Take a quick look at the table of contents for this book. The concepts of each chapter include things a PMO would have addressed for you. Without them, you will need to consider how you will build that component for yourself. Also, how you will build the infrastructure that will connect that component of your project to the organization around you. Without a PMO you will have to invent all this on your own, or with the support of your governance team.

We will talk about the governance team in Chapter 4. For the moment, consider them your managerial oversight and guide. You will need to work with your management team (and the project sponsors) to develop the oversight team appropriate for your project. Then, absent a PMO, they become your best advisors on what your project needs to consider. Their experiences and organizational insights can help guide your project through the challenges of your organization.

---

### Example
Planning a business trip to meet a prospective client

This time, imagine your company has no one in charge of customer contact. You are still going to have to make certain the appropriate people are supportive of your efforts. You will need to find flights, rental cars and hotels that are considered appropriate for your organization. If you engage in any negotiations with the prospective client, you are still going to have to make certain the agreement complies with the legal commitments your organization is willing to make. You will want to find some way of reporting to others about the contact you made with this potential customer. You are still going to have to do all the things an oversight department would have done for you. If you try to figure this out on your own, odds are the first time out, you are going to make more than a few mistakes. But, if you enlist the advice of your management team and those with some experience, you are more likely to be successful – especially in the eyes of your managers.

## Summary points

- A project manager's function occurs within the context of an organization. Simply driving tasks to closure is not sufficient; a project manager must make their project successful within the constructs of the organization about them.

- Often organizations establish a Project Management Office (PMO) that provides many resources. While there are different types of PMOs, one thing all PMOs do is establish where the project manager fits within the organization, and how they operate within the context of the organization.

- Every PMO will be different. It is unlikely a PMO will exactly fit just one of the discussed models. However, four broad types of PMO are:

  - supportive PMO;

  - directive PMO;

  - controlling PMO;

  - no PMO (everything is handled by the project manager).

- If you have access to a PMO, you should use anything they can give you. They will know about unique pitfalls, help you avoid previous mistakes of others, and possibly enable you to use and copy what was previously successful.

- If no PMO exists, you must still address all the things a PMO would have done for you.

# 04
# Project governance

All organizations have operational ways in which they function. The way in which an organization controls its functions
is called *governance*. Work outside of or in opposition to those
controls, and you violate the organization's governance. Because
all projects exist within an organizational context, the organization's governance defines whether your project is a failure (despite
any good you may have done), or a success (despite anything that
may have gone wrong). Thus, establishing proper project governance is a key factor to determining the success of a project. It is
the project governance team who determines whether or not your
project is successful!

You might think that if project governance is so important, it
would be a well-studied field, with commonly accepted best practices that we could follow. As the PMI practice guide on governance points out: 'There is no consistent approach to... project
governance... There are multiple definitions of governance in the
literature and standards; confusion exists in distinguishing among
the governance needs' (PMI, 2016: 3). You will need to find out
how your organization handles project governance, and work within
that context.

To help frame your thinking, we will look at the most common
project governance issues that one needs to address. Clearly, given
the preceding, what follows cannot be definitive. Build on what
you find helpful.

We will focus on the following aspects of the governance team:

- Their role as a guide for navigating organizational rules, customs and other such nuances.
- Where they and your project fit in the organization.
- The corresponding functions of the team.
- The form of the team (for example, the classic roles found on the governance team).
- Some operational considerations for working with a governance team.

Just as every organization is unique and every project is unique, the governance team for your project will also be unique. Despite the sense of academic ambiguity around governance team definitions and standards, in practice, working the basics and proper use of them will make them a primary asset to your project.

# Governance team guidance

A popular perception (of comedies, political satire and watercooler grumblings) is that corporate governance decisions are fickle, capricious, illogical or out of touch. These perceptions come from 'outside' the governance team (if you will); from people who see only a fraction of what was considered when an organizational decision is made. In reality, well-run governance teams typically make good decisions when one considers the overall organization. If their decisions were not typically good, then organizations would quickly go out of business! Understanding this context and leveraging this guidance is important to the success of your project.

## *Shadow governance*

Most organizations have an explicit form of governance. This consists of the documented rules, practices and methods by which the organization controls its functioning. Despite how complex or lengthy these rules may be, they are both explicit and finite, because they are documented. In theory, you could know them all, and design your project to comply with them all – meaning that the organization would find your project successful. However, there are also the implicit or unwritten rules. The problem becomes knowing when to apply which. Do not make the mistake of thinking that just because the unwritten rules are not documented, they don't count.

Every organization has undocumented understandings or norms by which some things function. Business process consultants refer to such things as 'shadow processes' because they occur in the shadows, so to speak. The documented rules govern most normal situations. Rare and unusual situations often fall outside the explicit processes. Still, the organization may have accepted ways for addressing the rare and unusual. Or, things are so well accepted that everyone just knows what to do even without documentation. People in organizations accept shadow processes even though such methods are not *explicitly* part of the organization's functioning or documentation.

If there are shadow processes, then, we might also talk about the existence of a shadow governance. Don't worry, we are not getting into the realm of some new spy-thriller novel. Shadow governance simply means the process by which the organization tolerates, manages or controls the shadow processes. For example: a practice or process that violates documented rules might in certain circumstances be considered acceptable, but only in understood special cases. Shadow governance is the means by which the organization retains control of the unwritten rules and processes; how it keeps shadow processes from going too far, or causing irreparable damage to the business.

## Being a special projects manager

Sometimes, by design, there are special projects (or departments, or groups), which are granted freedoms to function outside normal procedures. Special projects have unique demands, methods and practices that a project manager must address. Despite any lore you may have heard about rogue departments bringing in a project that saved the company, the truth is that even special projects are subject to oversight; they still must exist within the organization they serve. Projects that are truly ungoverned must either be quickly brought under governance control, or they typically must be declared failures by the organization regardless of what they did, good or bad, in order to preserve the long-term life and coherence of the organization. In the real world, special projects are not a licence to run wild. To be successful, the project manager must still fit the special project into the organization's governance structure, even if that is a 'special' governance structure for controlling special projects.

Managing special projects is a study unto itself (beyond the scope of this text). If you are a project manager over a special project, additional research is advised. I would start with *Kelly's 14 Rules and Practices*, developed by Kelly Johnson for Lockheed Martin's famed special projects division; it's widely recognized in the industry as being a good representation of special governance (Johnson, 2018). Many companies and authors have developed their own take on this model.

## *Explicit, implicit and more or less strict*

When we think of shadow governance, we may envision *relaxing* normal rules. However, there can be special situations that *heighten* the normal controls. Projects for that *sensitive* client may require a form of shadow governance that goes beyond the governance norms for the organization.

If you're now thinking this whole thing seems impossibly complicated, don't worry, you wouldn't be alone! Fortunately, governance teams seem to have a good track record for sorting through these nuances. This is why we say the 'governance team' embodies or represents the organization's governance. As a project manager, we do not try to understand all the rules and nuances that govern an organization. Rather, we assemble a team that collectively understands these things, and apply their insights (Figure 4.1).

**Figure 4.1** Guidance provided by the project governance team

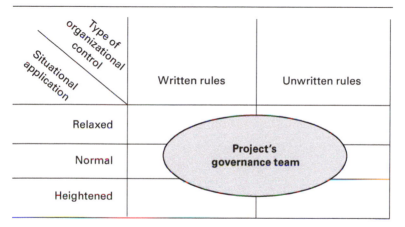

When looking at Figure 4.1, remember unwritten rules might be more or less stringent than the written rules. Unwritten rules may even address how and when the organization applies the written rules. The unwritten rule column could easily be three columns: application guidance for the written rules; when to be flexible; and when to invoke super-rules. So, while the figure is a simple 3 × 2 matrix, one could easily grow this to a 3 × 4 matrix, and maybe beyond. We won't detail each intersection of the matrix. Still, you might find it helpful to think of the written and unwritten rules used in everyday situations. As you go through your day, try to fit situations into this framework. How and when do the written rules apply? How and when do the unwritten rules apply? Real organizations function within this type of governance complexity and nuance. For your project to be successful, it must navigate this complexity.

To navigate this complexity, it is important that the project manager staff the project's governance team with people who have insights on the organization's overall culture. Where others may see illogical contradictions, this team will see clearly how your project needs to address each situation, based on their experience, insight or perspective (they are not advising from theory). By working with them, collectively, you and the members of the governance team can develop insights greater than the sum of the individuals; they can effectively guide the project through the organization's nuances and proverbial landmines.

# The project's governance team: fit and function

It is important to know where in the organization the project's governance team fits, so that it is appropriately staffed. In organizations of some size, other projects are happening in parallel. Besides the project work, there is the general operation of the organization's business. Projects, by definition, are temporary efforts. Hopefully, your business or organization is an ongoing endeavour. So how does all this fit and function together?

If your organization has a PMO, connect with them. They will have information that answers this question for your organization. Be aware that there are many views on this topic, and no definitive answer fits all situations. Some models for organizational project governance integration are quite different from what I will outline here. But in general, for most situations, there are some common themes for how a project's governance is integrated into the overall organization, and some common functions that a project's governance team typically provides.

For our discussion, I will assume a hierarchal organizational model. At the time of this writing, it is one of the most common organizational business models you are likely to find; plus, it simplifies our depiction. Even in other models, however, many of these same fit and function issues must be addressed.

## Governance team fit

Beginning at the top of Figure 4.2, we have the overall organization's governance. The responsibility and accountability for all that happens in the organization sits here. All information flows up to here. All direction for the organization comes from here.

**Figure 4.2** Project governance team fit and function

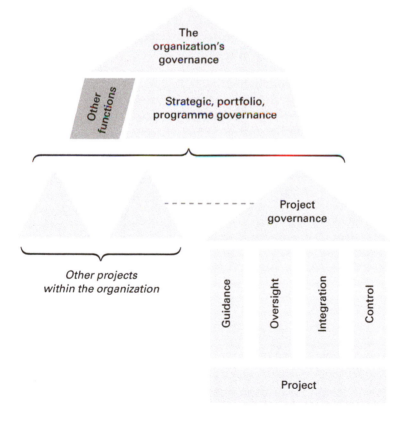

All the organizational functions unrelated to our discussion, we dump into that little box on the left labelled 'Other functions'. For this discussion, we can safely ignore them.

Right next to that box you see 'Strategic, portfolio, programme governance'. We will think of strategic, portfolio and programme governance as an oversight function for managing all projects within the organization. Depending on the size of your organization, this might be part of the lead executive's purview, or there may be separate management functions and support organizations for each, or any blend thereof. Their functions vary greatly by organization. Whole texts develop the concepts of corporate governance structures, strategic governance, portfolio management/governance, and programme management/governance. While all these are important topics for your organizations to address, you as a project manager simply need to be aware that these components are important inputs to the management of your project. Specifically, projects must fit within the overall:

- strategic considerations;
- portfolio considerations;
- programme considerations.

How that body functions is mostly irrelevant to you, except for their input to your project's governance team. Your governance team is accountable to these overall organizational governance decisions. So we draw the project governance team below the corporation's/organization's strategic, portfolio, programme governance operations.

## Governance team functions

By where we have placed the project governance team in the overall organizational structure, we can deduce another function for your project governance team: to determine how your project fits into your organization's strategy, portfolio and programmes. These things set organizational boundaries and goals for your project.

They will also define reporting requirements. They will set budgetary considerations, timelines, technology directions, and so on. All these things you need to know, because they are affected and defined by where your project fits into the overall organization.

The project's governance team supports your project's fit into this structure, through the functional pillars of project governance, as depicted in the bottom right of Figure 4.2. The 'pillars' of project governance vary across theories, models and organizations. Still, generally these four things mostly apply: oversight, guidance, integration and control.

## Oversight

A fundamental role of the project's governance team is oversight. They are the primary level of supervision, charged with monitoring the project as a whole. Despite the governance team being staffed by high-level organizational executives, odds are they do not have supernatural powers; the only way they learn about your project's progress is if someone tells them! Their function is to receive and understand the status reports that you as a project manager provide. Things that typically are of interest to them include: project progress, issues, challenges, performance, and so on.

As you form this team, work with them to determine a reporting format that gives them both the information you need them to have and the information they want to know, in the format that best communicates to this team. Remember: they are there to help you. If you do not keep them informed (especially of project difficulties, failings and needs) then they cannot help you. Keeping the project governance team effectively, thoroughly informed is critical to your project's success.

## Guidance

The governance team is also there to help guide the project to success. The focus of this team is the project, not you as the project manager. This is an important distinction to remember! A good, effective governance team will have insights that you as the project manager may not have, and your success depends on harvesting those insights. For example, if you tell them how your project plan will be approaching some facet of the project, and someone points out their thoughts on a better way to approach that issue, do not lose that possible wisdom! If you tell them you are experiencing a problem, it helps you if they work with you to solve that challenge. Our definition for a project is that the unaided abilities of one person cannot possibly manage it all. This team's counsel and help is your best opportunity to achieve more than is possible via your unaided abilities.

As part of guidance, we will add decision making. At times, the governance team may provide feedback to the project manager on how to address various things. Sometimes it might be more effective to use this team directly to resolve issues. For example:

- Project Scope Definition: in Chapter 5 we note a key role of the project governance team is to decide on and approve the project scope.
- Final budget, expense approvals and final timeline.
- Project acceptance: in many organizations, at the end of the project, this group will be responsible for accepting the final results of the project and closing it out.
- Change requests that occur during the project should be approved (or denied) by this group.
- Organizational resource commitments will be monitored and managed by this group.

As the project manager, you will be making many daily decisions. Some, you will float by the project governance team to keep them informed. For other decisions, you may seek their approval. However, there will be issues where their decision-making power and authority will be critical to defining the success of the project. The project governance team can be a great resource. Make the most of them!

## Integration

We have already mentioned upward integration: fitting this project into the organization's overall strategic, portfolio and programme plans. There may also be cross-organizational integration issues that need to be managed to make your project successful.

Often projects will have to reach out across many departments, or even other companies (say, for supplies, deliveries to external customers, etc). How the activities, staffing and information are collected, used and disseminated or reported is an important role of the project's governance team. Say you will be seeking help from some other department in getting your project done; the people from that department may need some involvement on your project's governance team. What is the appropriate level of involvement for them? You will need to sort that out. But the point remains: integrating your project across departments and other organizations is a key function of the project's governance team.

## Control

Here, we use the term 'control' to mean adherence to the relevant management plans, policies, regulations and the like (eg, compliance with the written and unwritten organizational rules, and even externally enforced regulations, rules, customs, and so on). How will your project objectively demonstrate (and document) the effectiveness of its compliance with these rules?

In this context, the governance team is responsible for establishing project controls and conducting appropriate project audits to assure these things are 'under control', or that the project is in compliance.

# The governance team: form

Knowing what the project's governance team is supposed to accomplish and do for you, now you need to staff the team. Make sure the people that you add to the team meet some key qualifications. Namely:

**1** They have an ability to speak for the component they are representing. You cannot have an effective governance team if the members have to check in with someone else before anything can happen.

**2** They are able and authorized to make commitments on behalf of the component they represent.

**3** They are there to make the project successful.

That last point may sound obvious. In my experience, there will often be people opposed to a project. Their goal of being on the project's governance team is to kill the project (and maybe they are trying to be subtle about it). Some classic project killer signs to watch out for:

- The assigned person (or critical participant) does not play well with others on the team. Being blunt: the rest of the team cannot stand them.

- The assigned person has zero availability. Assigning such a person to the project's governance team is a passive-aggressive way to slow down or kill a project.

- The project requires buy-in from a department that is implacably opposed to the project; their representative is typically a 'can't do' person. Now of course, prudence and caution are valuable at appropriate times. But appropriate prudence and caution from a project supporter will come with comments like '… but here is how you can address that problem' – in other words, they come with solutions as well as caution. Watch out for 'can't do' people assigned to the governance team.

If you see any of these issues developing, may I suggest that you try to immediately address this; preferably get someone else assigned to the team.

## Common roles

Now let's consider some common governance team roles:

- The **project sponsor**: This person is responsible to the business for this project. Often they have budgetary responsibility for the project; essentially, it is their money, or their budget, that makes this project possible.

- Practically, the project sponsor is often the **project champion** – but depending on the size and structure of the organization, it is possible that one person will be funding the project, while someone else promotes the merits of the project. In this case, there will be a project champion who 'embodies' the concepts, spirit, and motivational understanding for the project.

- The **Project Management Office representative** – depending on the role of the PMO in your organization.

- **Key stakeholders**: Typically, these will be representatives from any supporting departments, services or organizations. If you are going to use staff from other departments, then it can be helpful to have a person from that department on your project's governance team who is capable of committing resources to your project.

- **Customer representative**: This may actually be the customer, but it may be someone representing the customer's needs. For example, maybe it is inappropriate to have the actual customer in your meetings; maybe the project is developing something for a market (a 'virtualized' customer). Since a key job of the project's governance team is to approve the scope of work, requirements, change orders, and so on, if you do not have someone on the team speaking for the customer, then this team will not be effective in this aspect. Many good projects go awry because they forget about their customer.

- The **project manager** (you, of course).

> ## The golden rule
>
> Who chairs this group? This is a matter of some debate.
> Practically, the project manager knows what these meetings
> must cover; from a practical perspective, I tend to see this as
> being their meeting. However, remember the golden rule (he with
> the gold rules!); often it may be appropriate to have the project
> sponsor ostensibly chair the meeting, with the primary agenda
> item being the report and concerns of the project manager.

## RACI thinking

RACI stands for Responsible, Accountable, Consulted and
Informed. It is one type of RAM (Responsibility Assignment
Matrix – of which there are many differing types/philosophies).
Briefly, the technique involves plotting the project activities against
key participants, and assessing what type of role each person plays
for each activity:

- **Responsible** for doing the work. They may delegate the work,
  but it is their responsibility to assure that the work gets done.

- **Accountable**, or Answerable, for the correct and thorough
  completion of the task. To me, this is typically the management
  oversight for the task.

- **Consulted**: This is a person from whom you want to get more
  information regarding the performance of the task.

- **Informed**: This person does not have any actual involvement in
  the activity, but not keeping them informed could create
  problems later in the project.

While there are times and reasons to apply this method in detail,
when building a project governance team, I try to *think* RACI. I
review the activities, and first focus on who has *Accountability*,
from say a management perspective, for a particular task. That
management person is probably a key person to involve on the

governance team. Often, that manager will also be overseeing the people *Responsible* for doing the actual work. If not, then I may need to add to my team whoever manages those responsible for an activity.

Later, when we talk about project staffing, it will be the project's governance team that will need to get you the resources you need. Someone has to assign, to the project, people who will be doing the work. Someone needs to approve your requests for resources. Approving resources is one of the functions of the governance team, so you will want to make certain you have the people with the authority, ability and knowledge to do just that.

When considering an activity, it can be important to find out who needs to be *Consulted*; who has information about the activity that may be useful. You may not need these people on the project's governance team, but you may want to have them as guests at critical times when their input might help.

Participation in the governance team may not be static. Not all the activities happen at once. Likewise, not all the key people need to be involved in every aspect of the project. You may need to *phase* participation in the governance team to complement the current or upcoming activities of the project schedule.

This can create a proverbial chicken-or-egg type of problem: you'll need a governance team to help you determine when and who needs to be involved in the governance team. In real life, this problem is typically resolved iteratively. Work with the team you have (say, the project sponsor, initial key people, etc), and as you initially walk through the project with them, identify needed others. When, where and for what will their input be important? As you get others on the team, you may need their input to refine your governance team membership.

Lastly, there are people whom you will need to keep *Informed*. A classic cause of project kerfuffles is not keeping needed people informed. Typically, these people do not need to be on the project's governance team. Sending them minutes of the meetings, progress reports, key decisions and the like will usually suffice. Sometimes it is good to follow up with such people to make certain they are reading and understanding the information you are sending to them.

# The governance team: operational considerations

When establishing a governance team, you will need to define various operational considerations for the functioning of the team. For example:

- defining what is a successful team;
- running an effective and efficient meeting;
- building team rapport and building good working relationships;
- presentation and communication skills.

What makes governance team meetings successful (or not) are all the same things that make every meeting successful (or not) – except more so! Here's an illustration: I sometimes pause to estimate the full expense (benefits, salary, hidden taxes, health care and all other costs to the company) of the people in any given project meeting. Guesstimates of these numbers are good enough for this purpose. I add them up, and divide by 2,000 (a rough approximation of the number of working hours in a year). I then divide that result by 60 (minutes in an hour). The result is an estimate of how much each minute of this meeting costs the company. Put a few executives in a room, and the numbers quickly become staggering. If we also considered what these people influence, what else they could be doing… well, I think you get the point!

Often a project's governance team meeting is expensive to the organization. That is okay! This illustration isn't intended to paralyze or intimidate. The people on this team are there because they are key to the functioning of the organization. The expense of the governance meetings is a necessary expense, because the project needs their valued guidance. Our point: just like all meetings, it is important to do your best to get value out of these meetings.

(At this point, also see Chapter 13's section on upward reporting.)

## *A caveat unique to project governance teams*

For a project manager, managing a governance team meeting might be likened to herding elephants: most people in the room have more organizational power than you, and yet you have to corral them. You, along with the project sponsor (or whomever is the key executive over this effort), will need to have a way of working through those dynamics, deciding how to chair these meetings and so forth. Additionally, sticky moments are likely to develop around estimating the duration for the project, expenses/costs, resource needs or scope management.

In Chapter 8, see the section on 'Estimating the durations of the activities' with particular focus on the subsection covering the planning fallacy (Kahneman and Tversky, 1977). There we cover the reasons why these problems tend to develop. For now, simply realize that even experts tend to underestimate various components of the project, while believing their general perceptions are precisely accurate. The implication for you as a project manager is that when presenting such information, inevitably someone (possibly several people) will think that you have entirely, unacceptably, overestimated things. For these situations, special ground rules need to be set for the project's governance team. We will look at this more in Chapter 8, but here the invaluable takeaway is that when thinking about your project governance team:

> The whole team must, at the outset, agree on the methods, practices and procedures used for getting to a result. Then they need to accept the results that come from following the agreed processes. They must avoid their tendency to insert their general perceptions over researched, calculated, results.

Now it is valid for a team member to look at the method for getting to that result, and criticize the method. They may know a different method for getting that task done quicker, cheaper and better. That kind of scrutiny is good for the project! It will make your project run better if you can get all stakeholders to focus on the *process*, not the *estimate itself*. This will protect you from too many sticky moments, and (worse) from chronic underestimations of your costs, schedule and scope that are likely to come from people's 'gut' feelings.

On the other hand, if someone on the team looks at your results and they think *you* have underestimated something, that is a serious warning signal that you have probably missed something significant. Pay attention to their warnings, and reconfirm that you are not missing something about which they have insights.

## Completing the project triangle

In conversations about project management, many people focus on schedule and budget as if those were the only two concerns. There is a third, related component that is just as important: scope.

Project scope fundamentally drives the use of resources (ie, budget and costs) through the duration, timeline or schedule of your project. (For our purposes, we will use the term scope as synonymous with quality.) Old-school project managers will refer to these three things – time/cost/scope, or schedule/budget/quality, or some mix thereof – as the **iron triangle of project management**. Eventually, at some point during a project governance meeting, during a dispute on budget, quality or timeline, the classic project manager will be heard saying something like: 'Tell me any two, and I will tell you the third.' This is because the three things are effectively interrelated, just like the components of a triangle:

- If you have a fixed amount of resources and fixed amount of time, there is only so much you can get done. That is just the nature of reality.

- If you must deliver on a specified scope (and you cannot change the scope), but the resources/people available to you are also fixed, then the time it will take to get the job done is a result of these factors.

You are welcome to explore all the remaining permutations for yourself, but I think you get the idea!

The point is, everything we say about time and budget also brings with it an implicit conversation about project scope. Want to save money? Ask if cutting the scope is an option. Need to cut the timeline? Okay, what features can we leave off this version and include in the next? Always keep this relationship in mind when managing a project.

Thus, the key things the project's governance team must have jurisdiction over, and be committed to managing successfully, are:

- the project's budget/resources/support;

- the project's schedule/timeline/delivery date; and

- the project's scope/quality/features.

For the project to be successful, the project's governance team must collectively be able to rally organizational forces to address these issues, and it must have authority to adjust these issues appropriately.

## Summary points

- Governance is defined by the way in which an organization controls itself. Violate an organization's governance, and you violate the organization. If the organization's governance declares your project a success, then by definition, your project is a success.

- Commonly, the four operational functions the project's governance team provides to the project revolve around oversight, guidance, integration and control.

- Special projects are unique creatures. They are not ungoverned, just differently governed. Just like regular projects, the governance that defines them can determine their success or failure.

- Organizations are complex creatures containing written and unwritten rules that may or may not be applied depending on the situation. No singular unaided person can be expected to navigate this complexity. The governance team must guide the project through its challenges, which include managing the complexity of the organization's overall governance issues.

- The project's governance team must make certain its charter defines where in the overall organization's strategy, portfolio and programme this project fits. Typically, the higher levels of the organization determine this. If not, then the project's governance team should sort out these issues.

- The governance team must be staffed so that it represents all parties critical to the success of the project – and can resolve all organizational issues arising from the project. Watch out for people who might be 'project killers'.

- People on the project governance team are undeniably experts in their field. They are vulnerable to the planning fallacy. Set guidelines so that planning fallacy perception errors do not derail your project.

- The iron triangle of project management defines the critical issues that interact to define your project. The project's governance team must have jurisdiction over all of them.

## References

Johnson, K (2018) [accessed 27 December 2018] *Kelly's 14 Rules and Practices* [Online] https://www.lockheedmartin.com/en-us/who-we-are/business-areas/aeronautics/skunkworks/kelly-14-rules.html

Kahneman, D and Tversky, A (1977) *Intuitive Prediction: Biases and corrective procedures*, Technical Report PTR-1042-77-6, Advanced Decision Technology, Defense Advanced Research Projects Agency, Office of Naval Research, United States

PMI (2016) *Governance of Portfolios, Programs and Projects: A practice guide*, Project Management Institute, Inc, Newtown Square, PA

## 05
# Project scope

## Defining it, managing it, changing it and avoiding creep

**M**any think of scope as a statement of what the project will do: the results being sought, the specifications needed for compliance, the features to be included, the performance requirements that we will boast about, service levels to be achieved, and all the other positive things the project effort will be pursuing. While definitions like that have their place, we are going to take a utilitarian, restrictive view of scope.

For our purposes, scope means the limits, demarcations, boundaries and identifying features of a project.

Through this approach, we are better positioned to avoid problems later in the project. To us, the value of a project's scope comes from an ability to say *no* to certain things while saying *yes* to other things. The project scope becomes a foundation for decision making.

In this chapter we will focus on:

- defining the scope;
- getting buy-in; and
- change control (and limiting 'scope creep').

## Defining the scope

Think of project scope as a virtual fence. Inside the fence (in scope) is the land of *yes*. Outside the fence (out of scope) is the land of *no*.

If the project's scope simply stated or defined a goal, we might then ask what happens after achieving the goal. If achieving the goal is good, then is achieving a bit more than the goal better? And why not more after that? In Chapter 6, we will discover that this type of thinking actually creates customer dissatisfaction (despite popular intuition to the contrary). By definition, projects are temporary efforts. That means they must end! The scope not only defines the minimum achievements for the project, but also defines what the project will not do, the upper limits (if you will), where this effort ends.

It can be helpful to think of project scope like a legal contract; often the scope becomes part of a legal agreement. Just like legal agreements, there are many different templates available for drafting a scope. If your Project Management Office (PMO) has a template, or methodology, get it, learn it, become familiar with it and use it.

Still, some components seem common, and important, to include in all scope documents:

- assumptions;
- requirements;
- deliverables;
- acceptance criteria;
- limitations and exclusions.

## *Assumptions*

Assumptions are an important part of life. Making assumptions explicit is an important part of writing a good scope document. Put aside the fun clichés about what happens when you *ass-u-me* something; the reality is we all make assumptions all the time. We must! Making assumptions helps us get on with life. Mostly the assumptions we make work out, but when defining project scope, erroneous assumptions can be deadly to your project. Keep in mind that the easiest problem to fix is the one you avoid. One easy way to avoid project problems: making your assumptions explicit.

Every scope of work document needs to have an assumptions section. What goes in here? This takes some pondering, reflection and self-awareness. In real life, we often do not even know when we are making assumptions. The assumptions section asks you to be aware of things that are *typically* outside of your awareness.

Often the PMO's templates will include a list of assumptions, probably learnt the hard way on previous projects. Behind each of those seemingly odd assumptions is probably a good story! This is why in Chapter 14 we emphasize the importance of reviewing your project and taking time to improve your processes for the next project.

Even if you are building on an existing template, have your team review project activities for implicit assumptions. Typical categories include things such as:

- What **resources** are being assumed as available (people, materials, facilities)?
- Are there **financial** assumptions (cash flow, payments)?
- **Vendor** assumptions (delivery, credit terms).
- **Methodology** that will be used.
- **Technology** that will be available (software, platforms, access to network, computers).
- **Architectural** and **design** considerations.
- **Tolerances**.
- **End-user** consideration.
- **Geographic**.
- **Physical**.
- **Environmental**.

No such list could ever be complete. Each industry will have its own list. Every project manager will develop their own '*who-would-have-thought*' stories that become explicit assumptions on their subsequent projects. As you develop your scope document, access the generational wisdom of those with experiences on previous projects. Work with the governance team. When you think you are done – put this section aside for a bit. Then with fresh eyes, repeat the exercise. Involve your team. Get peer review. Ask those experienced in your industry.

---

### Example
Elevation assumptions

When you get on an elevator, you make a lot of assumptions. You assume the inspector found it to be safe. You assume the design includes systems to keep you from plummeting to your death, should something go wrong. I could go on, but you get the idea. Without making assumptions, you are not getting to your meeting on the 12th floor without being an athlete.

The problem is that when defining a project scope, making unsupported assumptions can be deadly to your project. Suppose you assume this elevator can carry to the 12th floor the equipment your company is selling to this client. What happens if, after the sale, you find out the equipment is too heavy for this elevator, and this building lacks a freight elevator?

The preceding is similar to a real problem I had to address for a supplier. The project scope statement failed to make critical assumptions explicit. Serious repercussions for many would have resulted without fortuitous creativity.

The easiest problem to fix is the one you avoid. Make scope assumptions explicit.

---

## Requirements

This section specifies what the project is required to do. Requirements need to be adequate, complete, accurate and unambiguous.

## Adequate

At first glance this may sound easy. But what does 'adequate' mean? The litmus test I use comes from concepts in patent writing. Namely, if the description is given to one skilled in the art (ie, someone of ordinary skill in the field that is being discussed), they would understand (without question) the work that is to be done on this project. If the description does not create a clear understanding, then the description is not adequate. Implicit to this litmus test: someone else, who is engaged, knowledgeable and critical, will be checking your scope document, and giving you feedback.

## Complete

While 'complete' is a simple word, you would not believe how troublesome this concept can be. Complete means absolutely everything. If it is not in the requirements, then we are *not* doing it. Often you might hear something like, 'In our industry it is just assumed that doing X also comes along with Y.' That needs to be mentioned in the assumptions! (On this point, also see the section below on 'Limitations, exclusions and things not included'.)

To make certain the requirements are complete, you may have to subdivide the section. For example, there might be system requirements, global requirements, user requirements, maintenance requirements, and so on, all found in the same project. Breaking the document into sub-requirements is often a useful strategy for making certain the requirements are complete.

## Accurate

Consider the project's requirements to be a dartboard. When you have finished the requirements document, does it direct all work to the bullseye? (And nothing else!) If the answer is yes, then you have accurate requirements. If the project has several targets – is that by design? If not by design, then fix it. If by design, be aware that the more 'targets' a project has, the more complex the project will become – making success much less likely.

## Unambiguous

Everyone brings their own history to reading a document. It is said that one can read Shakespeare at different points in one's life, and get different insights each time one reads it. Requirements documents are not supposed to be Shakespeare. We want everyone, regardless of who they are or when they are reading the document, to develop the same understanding. If another person will interpret the document differently, then you do not have unambiguous requirements. Get several people with critical eyes to review your requirements document. Classic guidelines for trying to make things unambiguous include:

- Express only one thought per statement.
- Avoid soft, catch-all terms, such as: appropriate, generally, not limited to.
- Avoid unverifiable terms: good, small, large, safe, user-friendly, easy.
- Avoid general conditionals, like 'when needed'.

When your reviewers raise questions about what something means, listen to them! Just the fact that they asked a question about something is an indicator that that section may need redrafting. Taking time here to critique and edit the requirements document will later save your organization much trouble and expense.

## *Deliverables*

Deliverables can be almost anything. Academics call such things widgets. A widget is a hypothetical unit of production. A widget can be a tangible object, a product, a service, a desired result... it is a generic term for talking about the *whatever it is*, or *thingy*, we are producing. Defining your widget(s) is a key part of defining your scope.

## Work breakdown structure (WBS)

If a project's scope is defined by its deliverables or widgets, a widget may in turn be defined by its components. The components might then be further deconstructed and defined by their constituent parts. You can imagine how this process could continue until we reach the activities that support the creation of our widget – similar to the level of granular detail needed for your project schedule (see Chapter 8). Breaking down a problem this way is generally called hierarchical decomposition. It can lead to a common project management tool called the work breakdown structure (or WBS).

If ever you have taken something apart with the intention of putting it back together, you know it is important not to lose any of the pieces. The same is true with hierarchical decomposition. As you create the next level in your decomposition of your widget, that new, more detailed, level must capture 100 per cent of what it takes to deliver the preceding level in the hierarchy. For this approach to succeed, you cannot lose any parts as you decompose your widget.

WBS decomposition is a nice theoretical concept; however, we know that anytime you are asking people to be 100 per cent sure about anything, there is a potential for problems. Still, in practice, with team support, reviews and attention to detail, it is a powerful method in a project manager's tool kit.

## Traceability

One of the benefits of using a WBS-like approach in your project scope and schedule is a concept called traceability. Throughout the deconstruction of your widget, contextual links between components or activities develop. The order of assembly becomes explicit; the links between dependent components or activities become obvious, and so on. Once you assign resources to the activities of the project schedule, you can then develop a complete project chain, linking any particular individual's contribution to the successful outcome of the project. This is traceability: the ability to trace every feature in a widget to an activity, a person or team responsible for developing it, and a requirement. Depending on your business, when your project is audited, being able to demonstrate such traceability can be critical.

## Going sub-atomic – how far to go with the WBS?

This begs the question, if you use the deliverables/WBS approach to defining your scope, how far do you decompose your widget in your scope document? There are many different views on this. The answer seems to be a blend between art, practicality and customer needs.

There are times when a full WBS including the detailed project schedule becomes part of the scope documents. This breakdown can also drive costing estimates, discussed in Chapter 11. I have worked on projects where before starting the primary project, the first thing that was done was to charter a *separate* project, where its scope was to create a WBS, project schedule and BOM (bill of materials) cost estimate for the primary project. Then that WBS and other material were used to create a business case and the scope documents for the primary project.

On the other end of the spectrum, sometimes only a high-level breakdown is included in the scope document. In these cases, it is felt that such a level of detail is sufficient for those familiar with the field to reasonably anticipate the subsequent levels of the WBS.

Anything in between these two extremes may be appropriate, depending on the circumstances. With the WBS method, the key is to remember your four requirements criteria: have you decomposed your deliverable to a level sufficient that your project understanding is adequate, complete, accurate and unambiguous?

Much is written about the WBS method and concept; we can trace its roots to the US Navy's efforts to project manage the creation of a Polaris nuclear submarine. Project managers have used the WBS concept successfully on large and small projects alike. We could talk about decomposition methods, common problems resulting from this approach, integration with other tools, and so on. In some industries, there are software tools that automate much of this method. Before you use this method, you will want to do some independent research on how best to apply this approach to your industry; find some examples of how your industry uses a WBS. For our purposes, we will use the term WBS to generically refer to the concept of hierarchical decomposition methods.

## Exercise
Practise the WBS

Think about a relatively low-stakes project for practising the WBS approach. This could be any smallish project from work or your home life; for example:

- building a new deck for your home;
- building your dream custom bike;
- planning a big holiday;
- planning an event, such as a work social or a birthday party.

Any relatively simple project will do. Pick something you can manage without a large team. Then try to develop the details for it using a hierarchical breakdown/WBS approach. The key is keep it *low-stakes, just for practice.*

Design a requirements document for this effort using a hierarchical decomposition/WBS approach as described in this chapter. What did you learn? Do you have a clearer sense of how this approach might be applied to a more complex project?

## *Acceptance criteria*

Acceptance criteria precisely define what is acceptable project performance and what is not acceptable project performance.

In Chapter 7 we discuss different lifecycle models. In some models, the acceptance criteria directly drive specific activities of the project. Whether the results of your project activities must meet their own acceptance criteria, or if the overall result of the project must meet a set of acceptance criteria, they will be a crucial part of your scope document.

The more you can make acceptance criteria specific, measurable and objective, the better off you will be. Avoid 'feel good' terms that are unverifiable. For example, who could argue with wanting to have your deliverable be user-friendly? But what does 'user-friendly' mean? One person's idea of user-friendly may be another person's idea of a wasteful nuisance. Common terms that are flags of trouble when found in acceptance criteria (besides 'user-friendly') are things like: flexible, easy, sufficient, safe, adequate, when required, fast, small, large... (take a moment to add to this list yourself, by considering words that sound good, but are actually vague or open to interpretation). If it is not clear what the term means (or if the same term can mean different things to different people), then trouble is on the horizon. It is best to be as precise and as clear as you can when defining acceptance criteria.

## Schedule and budget

There are those who will argue that schedule and delivery dates are not part of the scope document or your acceptance criteria. I understand that point of view. As discussed in the previous chapter, the iron triangle looks at the three distinct trade-offs that one must classically manage in a project: budget, time (or the schedule) and scope. Keeping these three things distinctly defined is a great thought... and then there is the real-world client.

To the real-world client, often delivery deadlines, milestones and key dates are defining components for the scope of a project. If your project misses these dates, you're outside the scope. The same is true for cost/budget; in capitalistic businesses, cost over-runs and budget overruns are definitely out of scope.

In the real world, you will need to complete at least some draft of the project schedule before you commit to the project scope, requirements and acceptance criteria. This is because you need at least a plausible demonstration that your team can meet the key dates and cost estimates/the project budget. If these things fail to meet the client's criteria for accepting this project, then the project is a failure. To meet the client's acceptance criteria for timing and cost, you might need to change other components of the scope document. These things must be fully understood before you lock down the acceptance criteria and overall scope document. This means that as a matter of practicality, various key dates and cost constraints are often part of the scope document – usually the acceptance criteria – even though they are distinct concepts in theory.

## Limitation, exclusions and things not included

Have you ever read that section of your insurance policy (or rental car agreement or something like that) labelled 'limitations and exclusions'? Certain exclusions need attention because in some cases one could buy additional coverage to undo that exclusion. Other exclusions just happen to be the nature of the industry, and I imagine there are interesting stories behind many of them!

The same is true of developing a scope document; it needs a limitations and exclusions section. While generally scope documents focus on what you will deliver, they must also define what you will *not* deliver. These boundaries help avoid scope creep.

Some considerations for limitations and exclusions might be: Are there any circumstances under which your organization needs to be released from delivery requirements? What might make per-formance of the scope untenable? What will force delays? Your organization's lawyer, if you have one, will also have their value in constructing this section. Typically, legal counsel will have catch-all words for the exclusion section noting something to the effect that if it is not explicitly stated, it is not within scope – that is, no additional aspects are implied. They will have other advice regarding exclusions and advice on other components of the scope document. See the section below on 'Involve your friendly organizational lawyer' for more thoughts on this topic.

# Buy-in

It is useless to craft the most beautiful scope document if it is not fully understood and supported. Elegance, compactness or other superficial mechanics are irrelevant; what counts is effective communication. The scope document is a vehicle of two-way communication: it first communicates to the customer the project's expectations. Second, it communicates to those who will be doing the work what they must do to meet those expectations. This is where the governance team discussed in the previous chapter comes in handy. As you develop the scope document, it is a good practice to review it with the governance team (since they are the management representatives of the people who will be performing the work).

Governance review of the scope document is often an iterative process. As you work with people in your organization on developing the scope, you may discover that other departments and representatives need to be included on the governance team. As additional people are consulted, components of the scope document may change, and the process may repeat.

The process of developing the scope document completes when all involved parties buy in to the scope. Getting a physical sign-off may seem a bit melodramatic (especially if this project is for internal consumption only). Still, a physical sign-off can be more important than you might imagine. In Chapter 8, we mention the value of sign-offs for creating cognitive dissonance and commitment to timing estimates. The same principle applies to developing the scope: before people physically sign off on something, they are more likely to confirm that they support it. After they sign off on it, they are more likely to support what they have signed, even when trouble begins to develop.

> **Tip**
>
> If the customer is external to your organization, it is probably important to have your organization's legal counsel involved. More on this below.

# Change control

The human desire to change things seems pervasive; a project without changes is the exception. Depending on the size and nature of the project and organizations involved, change control can be as much of a social process as it is an administrative process. Balancing these competing dynamics can be a real problem with change control. If one does not find the proper balance between the social dynamics and the administrative processes, relationships can be damaged or scope creep can become problematic.

Administratively, if your organization has a PMO they may have well-defined change control processes, forms, systems, databases, policies, and so on. Connect with them, leverage what they offer, and follow their guidance. If your organization does not have a PMO, you will need to develop an administrative process around managing change requests. Often, this will begin with the classic 'change request form'. You might customize a template from some other source to fit your needs.

Your change control process will also need to interact with your configuration management system to assess the impacts of the change (Chapter 10 discusses design and configuration management – but in a few words, your project needs a system to assess impacts of changes to the project's deliverables). Significant changes may also affect the project schedule plan, which will impact staffing, costs, and so on. All these things need to be considered when making a change to a project.

As project manager, your change control process must effectively review the total impact of the change: to the scope, to the schedule, to costs, to staffing, and so on. Textbook advice concerning change control typically suggests that one should never allow changes to the project unless the following standard criteria are met:

- The change is formally presented in writing.
- It has been reviewed by the governance team.
- It has been assessed by the project manager.
- Appropriate impact studies have been reviewed by all parties.
- The change request is formally signed and accepted.

There are many different ways of saying this, but the point is, everyone with relevant input and interests must buy in to the new situation, for without proper review, changes are often a source of project troubles.

## Change-ee troublemakers

A formalized change process can be seen as a deterrent to changes. Changes are typically expensive, and if not carefully assessed, unintended impacts can destroy a project. Because of this dynamic, tension can develop between whoever is trying to introduce a change (the 'change-ee' if you will) and the gatekeeper to the project – typically you, the project manager. If the 'change-ee' does not want to follow the defined process (because it is not to their advantage to do so), they become what we will call a 'change-ee troublemaker'.

There are many techniques change-ee troublemakers may use to get their changes into the project. The most common troublemaker dialogue I see starts with something like: 'Oh wait, this isn't really a change, this is part of what the scope includes… as I understand it.' Then there is the line that begins: 'Yes, but this should not cost you any more to do.' In general, it is bad practice for anyone associated with the project to accept anything that vaguely even hints of being a change. All official communications on such things need to be issued by the project's governance team. (Your organization needs to make certain the entire team supports you on this – you would be amazed at how people find sneaky ways to introduce changes.)

*All* proposals for changes need to be reviewed by the governance team. The governance team needs to consider if the change is in scope or out of scope and the impacts of the change on the overall project, business case, and so on (the project manager typically coordinates developing most of the related information the governance team will review). Then, if the change is accepted, it is their job to manage the financial impacts, resource impacts, and so on. Likewise, if not accepted, it is their job to manage the relationship with the change-ee.

Saying *no* to a change-ee troublemaker, and preserving the relationship with them or their organization, is not as easy as it might sound. While saying *no* is often the right thing to do to save the project from scope creep, an improperly managed *no* can also destroy relationships. For this reason, the governance team may sometimes decide to say *yes* even when the change request should be declared out of scope; or they may allow certain requests to short-circuit the process – which is their prerogative. If the project sponsor is especially powerful, telling them *no* can be fatal to the project in other ways, as well as to the career of the project manager, or even other people on the governance team. Balancing that dynamic is not trivial.

While no one rule fits all situations, in general I have found that usually someone on the governance team will have the skill and art of managing such social dynamics – or at least the management clout to do so. Bottom line: corral the change-ee troublemaker into following the process, and then let the governance team do what they do best, so you can do what you do best.

## Managing scope creep

There are many different types of scope creep:

- Sometimes a component of the project develops 'add-ons' that by themselves seem reasonable enough, but collectively the result is outside the bounds of the original scope definition.

- A part of the project discovers something interesting to pursue, and we can fit that extra work under this project; but such work is not part of the scope of this project.

- Someone spots easy wins that the project can seize for just a little more effort; the temptation of easy wins is a potent fertilizer for growing a project beyond its scope.

- We are all anxious to proceed, so we leave off that requirement and develop this short cut... yes, scope creep works both ways. We commonly talk about creeping growth of the scope. However, we can also have creeping justifications for not meeting the defined requirements of scope. Often, disasters can be traced to small justifications, adding up to not meeting a safety requirement or regulation; which grew into justifications to not comply with many other safety requirements or regulations; until the disaster was inevitable.

Before you know it, something that at one point did not even seem worthy of attention, or a small change that seemed totally reasonable or justifiable, now has the project on the brink of failure. Going unnoticed, small, incremental drifts or changes add up, eventually being a net major change.

One solution to this problem begins by checking all changes through a change control process. In that process, compare the changes to the original project scope and requirements definition. If, under the original definition, you see the current change as 'out of scope' then scope creep is at hand. The governance team must also confirm the change fits with the organization's strategic, portfolio and programme considerations. As discussed, the best thing to do is usually to say *no* and politely put the proposed change aside for the next project. If the change is something that the governance team feels may be valuable to do, it is usually best to build a new project around these new ideas. That is because once you say *yes* to something that should have been a *no*, your project will officially have the 'creeps' – and once the creeps start, they can be hard to stop. If no one on your team is able to say *no* – because of other social dynamics or organizational pressures – that is a good indicator that scope creep has invaded your project.

# Involve your friendly organizational lawyer

There are two ways to view project scope (and much of project management itself). First, your project is for an internal customer: your deliverables will be to or for someone in your organization or company. As long as everyone you are working with is also working for the same company, disputes can be settled within the overall governance of the organization. The other way to consider this material is that your project will be delivering something to an external customer. In this case, problems and disputes can have legal repercussions.

When considering the scope document, it is often said the best scope document is one that collects dust. That is to say, after it is drafted, the only person who uses it is the project manager (and maybe a few others) to define the work that is to be done. Other than that, it spends the rest of its time in a drawer collecting dust. The idea is that the process for developing the scope document was so good at making the project work clear to all involved that everyone knows what to do; and at project end, everyone is so happy that no one even goes back to look at the scope document to confirm what was originally required.

By contrast, when a project goes awry, the scope documentation becomes central to any dispute, along with any change orders. When doing anything that involves getting external customer sign-off on something, it can be smart and prudent to involve your friendly organizational lawyer.

After a while, project managers begin to feel that they pretty much understand the things that their lawyer will be scrutinizing. Great! That simply means the lawyer's review of your work will be that much quicker. Still involve them. This is their area of expertise; respect their skill and knowledge, as it is relevant to your project. You may become good at the routine stuff – but they have studied nuances, subtleties and rare peculiarities that by definition you might miss. Involve them on the governance team if they think it appropriate. Consult with them. Keep them informed. Follow their counsel. They are there to keep you, your project and the company out of trouble; help them help you, and everyone wins.

Your organization probably has rules about this, so my statements here are probably redundant. But if not, regardless of how familiar you feel with the topic at hand, resist the temptation to play lawyer; that becomes a problem waiting to happen.

## Summary points

- **Project scope** is the virtual fence that defines the territorial bounds of the project. Inside the fence that defines the project's scope is the Land of Yes; outside the fence that defines the project's scope is the Land of No.

- **Make assumptions explicit**: this is both difficult and crucial.

- The **requirements** define the project. This description must be adequate, complete, accurate and unambiguous. To ensure this, have someone skilled in the field critique your scope document.

- Often a project scope is defined by its deliverables. A hierarchal decomposition of those deliverables is called the **work breakdown structure** (WBS), a powerful tool for complex projects. Many project scheduling and project management tools can be linked to the WBS.

- The WBS facilitates traceability. **Traceability** is the ability to trace every feature in a deliverable to an activity and person/ team responsible for developing it, and also being able to trace all features to a requirement. This ability can be important when a project is audited.

- **Acceptance criteria** need to precisely define what is acceptable project performance and what is not acceptable project performance: avoid words that can have multiple interpretations. The more you can make acceptance criteria specific, measurable and objective, the better off you will be.

- As a practical matter, **delivery and other key dates** may appear in the scope document (usually under acceptance criteria) along with budget or cost limitations. As a result, often versions of the project schedule and budget must be completed to sufficient detail to make this possible.

- Because projects are temporary efforts, they must have bounds. The scope is also defined by what is **excluded**. Remember to include in your scope document a meaningful section on what is not part of this project.

- The scope document **communicates the intentions** of the project to both the customer and the team responsible for delivering on the customer's expectations. Getting everyone's buy-in is important. Typically, the governance team should represent all involved, and their sign-off should be a proxy for this buy-in.

- Change control is both an administrative process and a social dynamic. It is best to have a strong administrative process for all changes, and then let the governance team manage the interface to those trying to introduce changes.

- Eventually **scope creep** happens to everyone. Prior incremental changes can make new changes seem reasonable. Always compare all change requests to the *original* project charter and scope definition to see how far things have come. At some point, someone must be able to declare things have gone too far. If no one can speak up, then scope creep has probably invaded the project.

- Scope may involve getting sign-off from external people. Involve your **friendly organizational lawyer** to the extent they advise.

# 06
# The project quality plan

*There is no instant pudding!*

W Edwards Deming

W Edwards Deming (known for inspiring the Japanese postwar economic miracle, much of which was based on his quality principles) was a fan of pudding. While the instant counterpart apes its namesake, it is not real pudding; real pudding takes a bit of care to make, some skill, practice and time to cook. Deming was trying to make the point (Deming, 1986: 126) that quality does not come simply by appointing a few people, following a recipe and issuing edicts. Quality results come from skill, care, attention, learning... it is a confluence of many things that takes time to cook. The same is true of developing quality systems.

The project quality plan is a small subset of quality systems. For our purposes, it is part of the scope definition (see Chapter 5). Here, we will talk about some fundamental principles that support quality efforts: the idea being that if you use these principles as touchstones in developing your scope, project schedule, design, and so on – and develop a plan to address these touchstone concepts – that will make for a good project quality plan. Developing and applying these principles to creating a project quality plan for *your* project in *your* industry will take some personal work, insight, skill and time to cook. Of course, your organization's Project Management Office (PMO) may have their templates and guidelines that they will want you to follow; they can be a great source in developing a project quality plan that best fits your organization. As with everything in project management, always connect with your local PMO and make use of anything they can offer.

# Meet the customer's requirements

In the United States, Philip Crosby was a key figure in the history of developing quality programmes. A soundbite version of one component of his philosophy might be that quality happens when you meet the customer's requirements; no less and no more. The 'no less' part may seem obvious: if your efforts fall short of the customer's requirements, the customer clearly is not going to consider your project to be a quality project. The 'no more' part is not so obvious.

## *When is more not better?*

Despite popular thinking, more is not always better – and more can make things worse! If you go above and beyond the customer's requests, sometimes you may get it right and *delight* your customer. At the time of this writing, there is a trend in the field of customer service management that asserts that to create loyal customers one must *delight* the customer, by going far beyond their expectations. Reality is (ie, scientific studies show) that going above and beyond often creates dissatisfaction. While more might *sometimes* be better, if you try to take your project beyond the customer requirements, you are probably setting your project up for trouble.

In Chapter 5, we raised the idea that many people think that if achieving the goal is good, achieving a little more than the goal is better, and more beyond that. We saw how this view creates problems with scope creep, which can lead to expense overruns and project delays. These things will definitely dissatisfy your governance team, causing them to consider your efforts to be less than the agreed quality standard. If the governance team determines your efforts are less than quality, then it will not matter what the end customer thinks – your project is less than quality.

'*But what about the end customer?*' you might persist. '*Surely, if I can give them more options and do more for them, they will be happier customers, more loyal customers, and generate more customers for us?*' And you might think, '*If only I could persuade my Governance Team*'. For the sake of this discussion, let's say you can do all those extras at no cost, and still keep the project on schedule.

It turns out your good intentions can lead you astray. Consider the work done by Professor Barry Schwartz (2006). In developing products, people think that giving the customer more options and more choices will improve customer happiness and feelings about the product. Research shows this is not always so: Professor Schwartz found that too much choice can be overwhelming. Too many options can lead to customer dissatisfaction. Perhaps you may recall trying to configure a new product – an app, or new phone, for example – that had so many options, settings and choices, you were exhausted by the time you got it working. Your experience may be more typical than you might imagine.

Research done by Dixon, Freeman and Toman (2010) finds that attempts to 'delight' customers do not build loyalty. Rather, when it comes to customer service, helping customers solve problems quickly and easily does. My interpretation: hit the nail on the head the first time! All the extra attempts to delight the customer would have been efforts better spent on just getting things right.

This thinking is almost heresy to many. I will not belabour the point: everyone will have their exceptional example where *so-and-so* did *this-and-that* to delight a customer, and the results created more customers and loyal customers than expected. Indeed that may be so, but those examples are the exceptions: they are not reproducible or sustainable. By contrast, even though it may not be exciting, and may lack grand stories of Herculean efforts – if you hit the customer's proverbial nail on the head you will never go wrong!

## *Who is my customer?*

When developing a quality plan, you need to know who your customer is. Only that way can you know what the requirements are that you must satisfy. I am going to suggest your *governance team* is your customer.

There are two perspectives on this question. One says that to deliver a quality product you need to discover the end-user's wants or needs. This idea has merit. Some projects may include efforts for developing a report on end-user requirements. But, if the new product is creating a new environment, end-users might not be able to envision that new environment. Consider asking your great-grandfather for the requirements of a tech device you take for granted, which did not exist when he was growing up. When the end-user cannot envision the new environment, their input may not always be helpful, and may need some executive sorting.

The governance team will balance customer input against other considerations, such as: strategic plans, portfolio objectives and general operational concerns. Management's goals can differ from the user's goals. Management sees company developments beyond user needs. It is the responsibility of the management team to have studied their customers, collected such input and balanced all those things against corporate objectives.

Thus, no matter how you slice it, your customer is the governance team. Remember, you selected governance team members for their contribution and insight. As Chapter 4 notes, this includes a representative for the 'customer'/end-user. Circumventing your governance team to get input directly from end-users might be motivated by laudable goals, and yet, if not properly balanced against management insights and objectives, such an approach can set your project up for failure on many levels.

Because of this, in all cases, I recommend using the requirements as defined and approved by the governance team as your goal – no less and no more.

## Controls: How will you measure/validate that the requirements have been met?

Part of a good quality plan defines the controls that demonstrate you have met the requirements, or are on track to doing so. Good controls are objective, meaning the same result occurs regardless of who applies the control. Some people will say that controls need to be quantifiable (meaning the control measure yields a number): that perspective has merit, as numbers are easy to process, manipulate and analyse.

Still, I have seen many good qualifiable controls. A qualifiable control passes judgement on the thing being controlled. While that sounds problematic (judgements tend to be subjective), it is possible to make qualifiable controls that are objective and repeatable. A trite example might be that after three years of no car accidents, you qualify for a discount on your insurance premium. That is a qualifiable *and* objective control: your accident rate over three years is objective, and on passing that test, you qualify for the discount.

The key with controls is to first determine what needs to be measured. Sometimes you cannot measure the thing that you want to control or validate, but you can measure a proxy – such as in the car insurance example. Accident rate (an objective number) stands as a proxy for your quality of driving (a subjective judgement).

Here's another example: on your next visit to a doctor's surgery (physician's office), they may slip a sensor over your finger to tell them the oxygen level in your blood. They are not actually measuring oxygen in your blood, but rather they are measuring how your finger absorbs the light from the sensor. Some clever people figured out the relationships between the absorption of light and oxygen levels in your blood. They popped those relationships into a computer, and voila! The proxy is just as good as having measured the real thing.

However you define them – qualitative or quantitative – part of your quality plan should include the controls that demonstrate *objectively* that you have met the requirements.

By the way, controls and 'acceptance tests' are technically a bit different. Consider controls to be the broad overarching concept covering all measures used for monitoring the project. Acceptance tests are those specific controls that define what is acceptable to the customer. Practically, however, acceptance tests are often used synonymously for quality control measures.

## Caution: Proxy measurements can lead your project astray

In projects, unlike the doctor's office, you are rarely measuring purely physical properties. Generally you're measuring people's behaviour or results of their behaviours. Much is written about the Hawthorne Effect (so I will skip the details), but one conclusion is that generally people try to do their best (von Auw, 1983: 353–59). Sometimes, if the worker's view of what they think you want differs from the manager's view, odd behaviours result. The potential for confusion increases when using proxy measures.

I have no way of confirming this old story, passed on to me by a professor whose name I forget, but it makes a great point even if it is not true. So I will share it with you.

During the Cold War, the Soviet Union and the United States were constantly competing about various things. The nuclear bomb gap: who had the most tons of explosive power? The navy ship gap: who produced the most tons of war ships? This continued into just about every field. In some bureau in the Soviet Union, a director noticed that there was a farm equipment gap: the United States produced more tons of farm equipment per capita than the Soviet Union. This was a problem! How could Soviet farmers compete with Americans if they did not have enough equipment? All at the bureau agreed that this was a national crisis; the bureau chartered a five-year plan to close the gap. The basic requirement of this project was simple: help the Soviet farmers compete by sending them more farm equipment. The directors chose a proxy measure to track success: they would track the 'tons' of farm equipment produced. Their goal became to produce more tons of farm equipment per capita than the United States. As the project neared the end of its five-year plan, they were lagging behind. The project manager ranted to the team, this is a matter of national pride! We must beat those Americans and produce more tons of farm equipment than they do, or heads will roll! Fortunately, the project succeeded. No heads rolled. The USSR was now shipping to their farms more tons of farm equipment per capita than the United States sent to their farmers. Pleased with themselves, the directors took a victory tour to see all the farmers they had helped. As they went from one farm to the next, they soon observed the lead weights that the farmers had removed from the equipment. Clearly, this project had met its proxy measure of shipping to farmers more *tons* of equipment, but they had not met the project requirement of helping the farmers; the factories simply added lead weights to much of the equipment.

Moral: be careful what you measure! Your team will give you what you are measuring, but will that give you what you want? Make certain they know what you *want*. If using a proxy measurement, make certain they know the measurement is a proxy for the goal; that the goal is still the point of the project.

## Traceability/RTM

A good project quality plan shows traceability. As mentioned in Chapter 5, traceability means that every requirement is traceable to an activity (or set of activities) that is responsible for bringing about that requirement. This shows you have an action plan for delivering on that requirement. Also, the traceability plan will link the controls or acceptance criteria (mentioned above) to the requirement that they assess – showing that you can validate the project delivered on the requirement. The quality plan's traceability section is often called the requirements traceability matrix – or RTM section.

The links between requirements, and the activities, controls/acceptance tests, are often visualized as a matrix (more on this below). This not only shows that activities cover all requirements, but also that controls/acceptance tests validate that the project successfully met the requirements. (This is why we consider the project quality plan to be part of the scope document; we want the customer to sign off on the controls/acceptance tests as validating that the requirements have been satisfied.) The RTM should demonstrate a few key things:

- All requirements are supported by a set of activities (ie, there are no orphaned requirements).
- All activities of the project are happening to address a requirement of the project (ie, there are no orphaned activities).
- Some control or test validates delivery of each requirement for the project.

## Is the RTM really a matrix?

A purist creating a traceability matrix would list the entire set of requirements across one side of a grid, and all the activities along the other side. Then they might mark Xs on the field of the matrix showing where the connections between requirements and activities occur. In the real world, such a matrix quickly becomes unmanageably large, with a lot of white space in it (mathematicians call this a sparse matrix). Figure 6.1 is an example of RTM. Notice that many of the cells of the matrix are empty. Also notice that with any significant list of requirements vs development activities and acceptance tests, this grid quickly becomes huge!

There are alternative ways to represent sparse matrices. One common way is to create a table that specifies just the elements of interest. We could create a table where the first column references the business requirements document (BRD) number. The second column would reference the supporting functional requirements document (FRD) [this is another common type of hierarchical decomposition]. The next column references development efforts, and the last column lists the applicable acceptance tests. See Figure 6.2.

**Figure 6.1**    Example RTM drafted as a sparse matrix

| Module Development | Acceptance test | Reservations BRD 1.X | | | | | Orders BRD 2.X | | | | Bill Pay BRD 3.X | | |
|---|---|---|---|---|---|---|---|---|---|---|---|---|---|
| Business Requirement Document (BRD) reference → Functional Requirement Document (FRD) reference | | FRD 1.1.1 | FRD 1.1.2 | FRD 1.1.3 | FRD 1.2.1 | FRD 1.2.2 | FRD 2.1.1 | FRD 2.1.2 | FRD 2.2.1 | FRD 2.2.2 | FRD 3.1.1 | FRD 3.1.2 | FRD 3.2.1 |
| Module Development 1.1 | Acceptance 1.1.1 | X | | | | | | | | | | | |
| | Acceptance 1.1.2 | | X | | | | | | | | | | |
| Module Development 1.2 | Acceptance 1.1.3 | X | X | X | | | | | | | | | |
| | Acceptance 1.2.1 | | | | X | | | | | | | | |
| Module Development 2.1 | Acceptance 1.2.2 | | | | X | X | | | | X | | | X |
| | Acceptance 2.1.1 | | | | | | X | | | | | | |
| Module Development 2.2 | Acceptance 2.1.2 | | | | | | | X | | | | | |
| | Acceptance 2.2.1 | | | | | | | X | X | | | | |
| Module Development 3.1 | Acceptance 2.2.2 | | | | | | | | | X | | | |
| | Acceptance 3.1.1 | | | | | | | | | | X | | |
| Module Development 3.2 | Acceptance 3.1.2 | | | | | | | | | | | X | |
| | Acceptance 3.2.1 | | | | | | | | | | | | X |

**Figure 6.2**    Example RTM drafted as a table

| Business Requirement Document (BRD) reference | Functional Requirement Document (FRD) reference | Module development effort reference | Acceptance test reference |
|---|---|---|---|
| Reservations BRD 1.X | FRD 1.1.1 | Dev 1.1 | Accept 1.1.1 / Accept 1.1.3 |
| | FRD 1.1.2 | Dev 1.1 | Accept 1.1.2 / Accept 1.1.3 |
| | FRD 1.1.3 | Dev 1.1 | Accept 1.1.3 |
| | FRD 1.2.1 | Dev 1.2 | Accept 1.2.1 / Accept 1.2.2 |
| | FRD 1.2.2 | Dev 1.2 | Accept 1.2.2 |
| Orders BRD 2.X | FRD 2.1.1 | Dev 2.1 | Accept 2.1.1 |
| | FRD 2.1.2 | Dev 2.1 / Dev 2.2 | Accept 2.1.2 / Accept 2.2.1 |
| | FRD 2.2.1 | Dev 2.2 | Accept 2.2.1 |
| | FRD 2.2.2 | Dev 1.2 / Dev 2.2 | Accept 1.2.2 / Accept 2.2.2 |
| Bill Pay BRD 3.X | FRD 3.1.1 | Dev 3.1 | Accept 3.1.1 |
| | FRD 3.1.2 | Dev 3.1 | Accept 3.1.2 |
| | FRD 3.2.1 | Dev 1.2 / Dev 3.2 | Accept 1.2.2 / Accept 3.2.1 |

As you can see, the table is easier to manage, can be included in reports, and can be used for designing databases. By custom, it does not matter how you show the relationships. Any method by which one demonstrates this information is called a Requirement Traceability Matrix (even if not presented as a matrix), because in theory, a full matrix could be constructed using the information.

I have seen software tools for managing this concept in large projects. Your PMO may have their own database tool for working with these things. With modern database creation tools, many people develop their own customized databases to address unique project needs. As we discuss in Chapter 10, you may want to add a key features element to your traceability database. Still, I have also seen many large projects successfully manage their RTM via simple spreadsheets and word-processing templates. Use the tools that you find helpful, but do not get hung up on the tool. The tool is not the thing that counts. Being able to follow and use the relationships between the requirements, activities and controls/acceptance tests is what counts.

In Chapter 9 on the project staffing plan, we assign staff to activities. The traceability matrix enables us to know that appropriately qualified people are working on the tasks: people who are capable of addressing the requirement that is supported by that activity. We'll discuss this more in Chapter 9.

# Small mistakes enable big successes (aka prototyping)

I have heard it said that our most valuable lessons come from our mistakes. Yet if mistakes happen on a large scale, they can be devastating and irrecoverable. Suppose we could find a way to make our mistakes happen on a small scale, and apply those lessons learnt on a big scale. Then our successes could be big!

There is. It is called prototyping.

One quality tool brought to us by W Edwards Deming (the influential pudding fan) is the Deming Cycle – sometimes referred to by the initials: PDCA (Plan, Do, Check, Act/Analyse) (Deming, 1986: 88). In Chapter 7, we look at a whole lifecycle model based on this idea, called the rapid prototyping lifecycle. Whether you are using that lifecycle model or not, there will be moments in every project where something is not perfectly understood.

A good project quality plan will look at a project for possible points where misunderstandings, goofs or simple disconnects could cause problems: the high-risk components of the project. If something goes wrong at these points, the impacts could be devastating. As you review each of these areas, ask if prototyping could help avoid problems. If so, build into your project quality plan a prototyping phase – an experiment of some kind – to prove the details (see Chapter 7). Then learn from those mistakes, so that you do not repeat those mistakes in the overall project.

In other words: develop a quality plan that includes prototyping so you can make your mistakes small, enabling your successes to be big!

# Design for tolerance of variation and interactions

Much in quality systems engineering focuses on reducing variations of all kinds; variation is the enemy. Why? To project managers and quality engineers, the term **variation** means the difference between the *ideal or expected situation* and what actually happens. Of course, we want what happens to be as close as possible to the ideal. Making things repeatable, predictable and reliable are important aspects of any quality plan. In developing your project quality plan, look for places where you can reduce variation.

Many discuss the importance of reducing variation in received raw materials, supplier-provided components, processes, delivery dates, and so on. If others provide you with quality goods and services, it makes your job much easier. In a book, it is easy to write that you should ask your suppliers to reduce the variation in what they give you! That might mean using tighter tolerances, or other premium considerations, when sending specifications to your providers. Stepping outside of the book, we quickly discover that tighter tolerances and premium considerations typically come at a higher expense to the project. This begs the question: are those requests for improved quality really worth it? We'll come back to this thought in a moment.

Despite all attempts to reduce sources of variation, in reality: everything still varies! To make it worse, things also interact. Even though something happened one way once, under difference circumstances a different result may happen. Projects can have unique variations of their own. That delivery which generally arrives in 30 days might take 45 days during winter months. During the summer months, holidays may change the availability of resources. The Heraclitus cliché points out that no one ever steps in the same river twice, because the river changes and so do we. Everything is always changing. How these changes interact can make results vary, despite all your efforts.

Good project quality plans also look for ways by which the project can accept variations and still manage the project reliably to a quality conclusion.

You might see a balancing act developing:

- On one hand, we need to reduce things that introduce variation to our project and activities.
- On the other hand, reducing some sources of variation will cost me more money.
- But, despite all my effort, some things will still vary.
- My project will have unique variations of its own.

Despite all this, I have my deadlines and budget restrictions to meet. How do I sort all this out?

## Cost of variation

Genichi Taguchi is best known for his statistical techniques, especially his concepts on designing experiments to learn about what is causing variations in products. His methods look at the interactions between variables. We will not go into his mathematical methods here, but one component of his work looks at the costs that happen as we vary from the ideal. As we minimize our costs associated with managing variation, the idea is, we improve the quality of our project – ironically at lower and lower costs. That is, it should cost *less* to have a higher-quality project, by paying attention to how much each quality control measure costs.

We can apply this to developing a project quality plan. For example, if variation in the completion date of an activity has no cost impact to your project, then that is not an area in need of attention. Good! But suppose there is a high-risk activity that occurs near the end of your project plan. A completion delay in *that* activity could delay the whole project, and cost your organization a lot. If you are able to schedule this same activity near the *beginning* of your project instead of near the end, then a completion delay in that activity could be fixed at a much smaller cost, without impacting the overall timeline of your project. Now, there may be extra costs for doing that activity upfront (maybe supplies need to be expedited). Quickly, we see there are trade-offs to consider. Is the cost of moving the activity forward smaller than the cost of the possible delays if it remains where it is?

Develop the scenarios that need to be explored. Estimate the costs of the possible outcomes under different circumstances. Then find a scenario that minimizes the total costs of the variations you are considering (the supplier costs, the costs to your project, and so on). The scenario that minimized the cost of variation is probably the optimal approach for your project.

For involved processes, Taguchi developed some nifty mathematical methods for sorting this out. However, for most project planning and scheduling purposes, with the right tools (which we discuss more in Chapter 8), usually some reasonably good solutions will become obvious. Modern planning tools will give you different visualization methods, and an ability to explore 'what-if' scenarios. They may even have other types of optimization tools, load-levelling tools, and so on. Using a good tool can save you a lot of time and maths.

Keep in mind that it is just possible that minimizing risks and minimizing variation could be more important to your governance team than the cost. Or maybe they are willing to accept some risks, because of conflicting schedules elsewhere in the organization. They may have a strategic perspective that might not be obvious to you. As you develop an understanding of the various trade-offs, it is important to make certain the governance team understands the costs involved between these trade-offs. They might have an 'executive prerogative' which transcends your analysis. That perspective is often more important than the maths. That is why the governance team is there.

# Regulatory and compliance plan

It is not consistent across industries where you put a section on regulatory and compliance planning. Some industries put this section in the requirements document. Others put this material in the quality plan. Others want it to be its own separate document. If your organization has a PMO, find out what they want you to do about this. Follow their advice.

If your organization does not have a PMO, ask around your organization and see what has been done on other projects. Ask people on your governance team. Do some research concerning what is appropriate for your industry.

The only point I am making here is that you should consider if the results or activities of your project might fall under the auspices of some regulation, regulatory body, code enforcement, industry oversight, and so on. If so, find out what those regulations and compliance issues are, and develop a plan for keeping your project in compliance as needed.

## Summary points

- Connect with your PMO, and see if they have any guidelines or templates or such that they want you to follow in developing your project quality plan. Use anything they can give you.

- Develop a project quality plan that shows:

  - You will meet the customer's requirements: no less and no more! Going beyond the customer requirements is often found to create dissatisfaction.

  - Every requirement is traceable to activities that support the development of that requirement. Likewise, it is good to show that all your activities are being performed for a purpose (ie, are linked to a requirement).

  - Every requirement is traceable to a control/acceptance test/criteria that will be used to validate your project's compliance with the requirement.

  - You have a plan for prototyping various aspects of your project, so you can make your mistakes small, enabling your successes to be big!

  - You have a strategy for minimizing the costs of variation, and the effects variations might have on your project.

- The governance team is there to balance many considerations, including end-user needs, organizational needs, expense needs, schedule needs, and so on. To make your project successful, consider them as your customer, so that all these needs are properly balanced.

- If your project is subject to regulatory and compliance issues, develop a plan for addressing these concerns.

# *References*

Deming, W E (1986) *Out of the Crisis*, MIT Center for Advanced Engineering Study, Cambridge, MA

Dixon, M, Freeman, K and Toman, N (2010) Stop trying to delight your customers, *Harvard Business Review*, 88 (7/8), 116–22

Schwartz, B (2006) More isn't always better, *Harvard Business Review*, 84 (6), 22

von Auw, A (1983) *Heritage & Destiny: Reflections on the Bell System in transition*, Praeger, New York

# 07
# Different types of project lifecycle models

In Chapter 2 we noted that projects are temporary efforts; they have a finite life. They have a beginning, a middle and an end. How will your project live out its life? What will be the models or philosophies by which your project lives?

In project management, there are different frameworks, models and philosophies for organizing project lifecycles. Find the framework that harmonizes with the work at hand, and the organization of work seems to sing. Apply a framework that is at discord with the work at hand, and with enough effort you can still accomplish your goal – but you are going to have to work a lot harder.

In practice, it is more complex than that. A project of reasonable difficulty, size, or which spans multiple technologies might exhibit different types of character simultaneously. Different types of project lifecycles might harmonize better with different components of the exact same project. If that is not bad enough, over time, a particular component of work might be better managed by a different lifecycle model or philosophy from the one you used for an earlier phase of the exact same component. In real life (as opposed to textbooks), you may find that you have to blend multiple strategies and models to manage the full lifecycle of your project.

To help you get a perspective on this, we will look at four basic project management lifecycles/philosophies. There are many writings and books on each of these, and on models not mentioned here; consider this a starting place, on which you can build by doing more research. Also, your local PMO may have published specifications on how they want you to apply these models (especially in government entities/projects). This chapter will cover the main characteristics of each, and point out which lifecycles might match which types of work. Then, when you are developing your project schedule (see Chapter 8), you can use the lifecycle components that give you the best approach for the type of work at hand.

The four lifecycles and philosophies we will discuss are:

- the classic waterfall/predictive lifecycle;
- the V-model;
- rapid prototyping (RAD)/the spiral lifecycle;
- the Agile concept.

## One size does not fit all

I have not seen one approach that fits all situations. Project managers are most effective when they blend lifecycles or methodologies to craft what works best for their organization, and for the activity at hand.

But remember: your position as project manager exists within your organizational context. For some organizations, it is important that you use a particular method – even if that means the project will take longer, or there exists other downsides. In situations like this, remember that success is impossible without the support of your organization. The 'perfect method' will not be successful if that 'perfect method' is not supported where you are. Finding that balance, between an ideal solution and the success that is possible, is what good project managers do.

# The classic waterfall project lifecycle

AKA the predictive method.

The so-called waterfall project planning lifecycle is probably the oldest, most natural form of project planning. As children, we learn that when building something, we must do some things first, after which other things follow, and so on. We can find this approach of sequential planning mentioned in our oldest cultural literature. (Even the Bible refers to this type of project management lifecycle!)

In constructing anything, the order of assembly is critical. Get this wrong, and problems follow. In project management, these problems can include project delays, and cost overruns due to rework (undoing work and having to repeat it). A common guideline is that rework caused by insufficient planning and reviews for construction projects adds about 25 per cent on average to the original timeline and costs.

---

### Try this

Search for current news stories, or think about events in your own experience, where a construction project had cost overruns. Were the cost overruns and delays due to:

- rework (having to undo and repeat work already done);
- changing requirements;
- or bad planning?

These three things account for most of the cost overruns on construction-type projects. Developing insights on other projects will help in managing your own projects.

## *Why is it called a waterfall?*

Start by depicting the sequential steps of a project as boxes, beginning in the upper left-hand corner of a page, ending with the last activity in the lower right-hand corner. Then connect the boxes with arrows showing the workflow. The depiction of the project might look something like Figure 7.1.

**Figure 7.1**   Sequential project representation

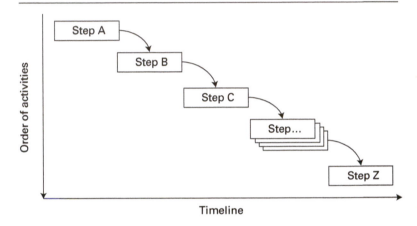

This type of project depiction has been around for some time. Someone thought this looked like water falling down a set of rapids; maybe the arrowheads are the splash as the water hits the lower landing. With that, they called this *the waterfall model*, and the colloquial term stuck. If you mention this term to just about any English-speaking project manager, they will know exactly what you mean.

When a project has these characteristics:

- you are able to gather adequate, complete, accurate requirements (to which everyone agrees);
- you have access to sufficient knowledge about what such a project takes to complete; and
- the project is *constructing* something in a physical/physical-like sense;

then you can follow these steps:

1 Gather complete **requirements** and get all relevant parties to agree on the requirements.

2 **Design** what it is you intend to build – and develop a plan for how you will build it.

3 Build it/**implement** your design.

4 **Validate**/confirm you got it right.

5 **Maintain**/deliver what you built.

Some texts may refer to this model as the predictive lifecycle, because you must start the project by predicting all the things that your team must do. When you can follow these steps, the predictive/waterfall lifecycle model is probably the most efficient, effective project model you can use. See Figure 7.2.

**Figure 7.2**   The predictive waterfall model

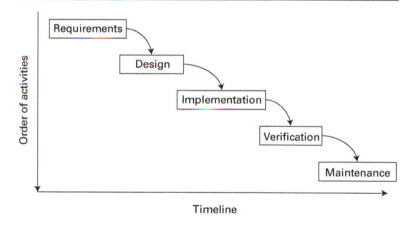

There are two key assumptions implicit to this model.

## Assumption 1

*That you are able to gather adequate, complete, accurate requirements – and get everyone to agree on those requirements*

You might think no one would start a project without knowing the goal. Go back to the opening scenario in Chapter 2; everyone thought the desired goal was clear, but no one had documented that understanding and got explicit agreement on that thinking. Often when people think there is unspoken agreement, it is likely everyone has a different thought on that agreement. A 2014 study by the Project Management Institute (PMI, 2014) found that 47 per cent of unsuccessful projects fail to meet goals due to inaccurate requirements – in other words, not having a clear and agreed to goal.

The waterfall lifecycle depends on having good requirements at the start of the project. For requirements to be 'good enough' for the waterfall lifecycle, they have to be grounded in reasonably similar experiences. The project manager builds on those similar experiences, or on such information, to detail the requirements document that defines the work of the project; you cannot 'predict' those things unless you have experience/benchmark information on which to base that prediction. For example, if you are building a house in a city where your company has already built many such similar houses, then getting good requirements should be rather straightforward. If, however, you wish to build a house on, say, the moon, you might not be able to get good requirements at the start of your project. In that case, this model is not well suited for such projects.

## Assumption 2

*That sufficient knowledge about what such a project takes to complete is available to the project manager*

This model requires that corporate familiarity exists with the components needed to complete the project. Your organization must be familiar with the kind of project you want to do. If no one has ever done anything like this project before, then you have no foundation for the estimates, plans or resource specifications needed to complete this type of project. In such a case, the waterfall model is not going to be very useful. By contrast, if this project is similar to 100 previous projects (or all the components of this project have components found in other similar projects, with which the project manager is familiar), then you will have extensive corporate familiarity about what goes into driving this project to closure. In such a case, it is possible to create reasonably accurate plans using this lifecycle.

Even though these assumptions may feel onerous, many things meet these expectations. As the cliché goes: there is nothing new under the sun! Often, the primary job of a project manager is to find previous examples that are reasonably similar to the components and steps that will be part of this project. Based on that information, they develop the lifecycle plan for the current project. Through research, study, making analogies, deconstruction, developing relationships, and all the other things a project manager will do, the assumptions of the waterfall lifecycle are often satisfied.

## Project management evolution

Prior to roughly 1950, this method rightly dominated cultural thinking, because then most things were physically constructed. In 1969, Ted Hoff developed the idea for the first 'universal processor', which gave birth to the first microprocessor (the Intel 4004). Obviously skipping a lot of detail, this invention changed many things – including the environment surrounding projects. There was something new under the sun!

As microprocessors found their way into nearly everything, software became a significant component of what got made. In some sense, software is captured thought. It is not physically constructed. People who create products that are primarily the result of knowledge and mental efforts, as opposed to physical efforts, we call 'knowledge workers'. Many modern projects occur in an environment driven by and/or somehow dependent on a component of software development, or that of capturing thoughts, or that of knowledge work.

The problem with capturing thoughts/managing knowledge work is that we do not develop thoughts in the same way we construct physical things. Thoughts often grow in response to a need. Thoughts might grow circularly. We might build our thinking from previous smaller thoughts, or have flashes of insight. Sometimes we need to think something through completely, see that we got it wrong, learn from our mistakes and start all over again (a disastrous process if you are constructing a building). Sometimes we need to bandy ideas about with others to develop our thinking. The processes for 'knowledge work' can be dramatically different from how we construct a thing.

For projects where software and captured knowledge are a major component, the waterfall model is not very useful. Attempts to apply this model to such things made it the epitome of project management schemes everyone loves to hate. Some refer to this method as 'the predictive method' while making the innuendo that since it is impossible to predict the future, this model is silly. This model is not silly; it simply is not the right lifecycle model for managing these types of activities.

## The waterfall model

To recap, this model is virtually ideal:

- when you are constructing something physical;
- when you have adequate corporate familiarity with or access to such knowledge about the goal and therefore you can develop good requirements; and
- when you have corporate familiarity with what it will take to complete the components of the project.

When these things are true, then the most effective, efficient, best way to model your project is to:

1  Develop good requirements for your project.

2  Design the thing you intend to build – along with the process for building it.

3 Implement your design.

4 Once you have finished building it, validate and confirm that what you built satisfies your requirements.

5 Maintain or deliver what you built.

# The V-model

The V-model is similar to the waterfall model, but our 'waterfall' becomes folded, with explicit connections between the final stages of the project and the initial stages of the project.

A classic feature of the V-model is that each development activity has an explicit connection to a testing activity that measures the success of the development activity. Every step comes in a pair – an activity/task, and a test of that activity/task. For a project manager using the V-model, defining these tests and associated criteria is a critical part of the planning stage. Knowing what these test criteria are, upfront, our knowledge workers can then hone the product of their craft to pass these tests. The theory is that if everything passes these tests, then you have created a successful product.

Let's build a V-model for ourselves, and see how this works.

## Start with the end in mind

Supposedly, a habit of 'highly effective people' (Covey, 1989) is to 'Begin with the end in mind' (Habit #2). Applying this principle to planning a project, we start by defining our customer's acceptance criteria. At the end of the project, when we hand our user 'Thing X', what are the properties they need to find in 'Thing X' for them to accept it as being successful? How we objectively test for those properties, we call user acceptance tests, or UATs.

Products have to be deployed, used and maintained. Therefore, at the end of a project, we also think about measuring deployment success, operational success and maintenance features. Often, when developing contractual agreements for delivering something, the contracts will refer to these criteria and metrics as 'service levels'. So in Figure 7.3 we begin building our V-model by creating these steps: the user acceptance tests or the acceptance criteria, and defined service levels.

**Figure 7.3**    The V-model – beginning at the end

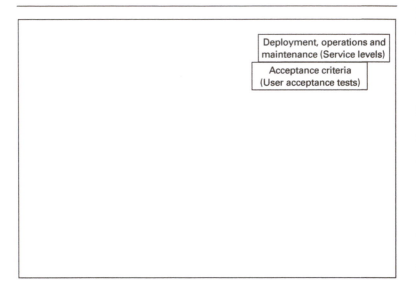

We use this understanding of customer acceptance to create our requirements. In practice, often the acceptance testing becomes the requirements. Despite this temptation, there is value in treating the *requirements* and the *acceptance criteria* as two distinct concepts. It is important to create a summary document that describes a high-level understanding of the project's scope, where this fits in our overall portfolio of product offerings, and so on. As discussed in Chapter 4, this information is important to the governance team overseeing the project (test criteria might not be as useful for their purposes). Each time we change our requirements, we need to use that new information to drive a change in our acceptance testing. Each component of our requirements must be demonstrated via some type of acceptance test, or, in this model, we will not consider that requirement or feature to be a valid requirement. Figure 7.4 depicts this concept.

You might ask, which gets created first: the product requirements or the operational/service requirements. That is a fuzzy issue. Sometimes the requirement document for a new product comes first and the service features follow. Sometimes the driving force behind many projects is an improvement to service levels. In this depiction, I have butted these two boxes up against each other to signify that they are really one thing.

**Figure 7.4** The V-model – specifying requirements

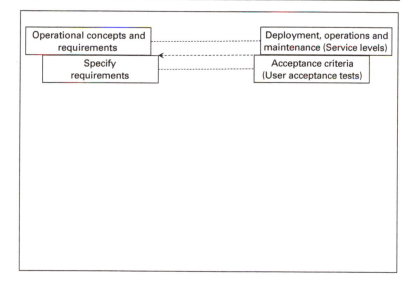

## Levels of design

Once we have our requirements, the waterfall model goes on to design and implementation. In the V-model we break 'design' into three hierarchical levels. We start at the highest level of understanding, and successively develop the details needed to support that high-level goal. We first create the high-level design or the architectural design of our product. We deconstruct that into the detailed design, answering the question: 'What are the structures needed to support our architecture?' To support the detailed design, we specify the components of those structures. See Figure 7.5.

**Figure 7.5**  The V-model – designing our product

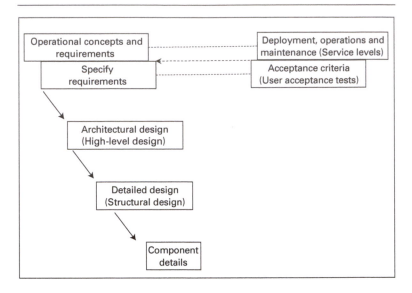

Remember the theme of the V-model is testing; specifically, what is the 'backend testing' that confirms the frontend work is acceptable? As we think about each design phase, we also think of their testing counterparts. At the component level – the most detailed level of design – we think of what tests or specifications each component must meet to be acceptable for use in our project. We call this step unit testing. As we put the units together, creating the structures of our design, what tests demonstrate we successfully brought the units together (integrated them)? This is called integration testing. Then we take those various structures and bring them together to create our system. Validating that the system of our structures is correct is called system validation. See Figure 7.6.

In software development, once you have detailed the components that the programmers must create, the next step is to have someone write the software that becomes those components; this is called coding. If this approach is used for things other than software, we might talk about procurement, craft creations, component development, and so on. For the sake of convenience in our diagram, we will simply insert a 'coding' box between the 'component details' and the 'unit testing' and generically refer to this step

**Figure 7.6** The V-model – how design steps relate to testing steps

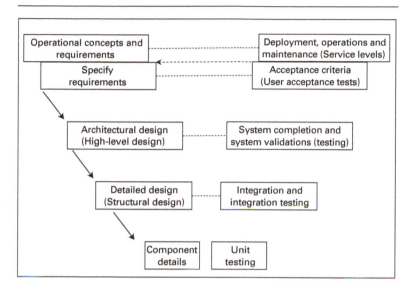

as implementation (others may use different terms). Now connect the workflow up the right-hand side of our figure, and the V-model is complete. See Figure 7.7.

**Figure 7.7** The complete V-model

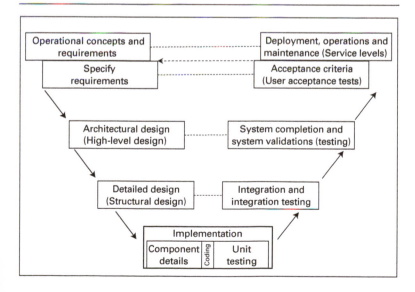

Ideally, the philosophy here is that before the design and knowledge work is done, all the testing requirements are defined. Then, as the knowledge workers do the work of each stage, they hone their efforts to create what will pass the backend tests. Then, as the designs are implemented, integrated, aggregated into a final system and deployed, the tests will confirm success. While our idealized model depicts a direct process, one point of testing is to find issues. On finding issues, rework will be needed. In practice, the model becomes iterative. When planning, allow contingency time for such rework. Benchmarks for rework vary by industry and company.

## *Uses for the V-model*

While most people discuss the V-model as applying only to software development, this model can apply to many forms of knowledge work.

### Example
Building a custom home

Imagine your project goal is to build a bespoke home. While many parts of constructing the physical building are, of course, construction activities, modern architectural work falls in the domain of knowledge work. For example:

- The customer will have tests they will want to do on the final house, to make certain it measures up to being their dream home.

- The architectural firm will transform the expression of these tests into requirements. Those requirements will support an architectural design.

- When the customer signs off on that high-level design, the architectural firm will create supporting detailed designs (construction documents that define the structures needed to make the architectural drawings a reality).

- Then those structures need components. A BOM (bill of materials) will be created, so that everything needed to build your dream house gets purchased and delivered.

- As components arrive, they have to meet certain component specifications.

- As the construction team builds the structures, code enforcement officials will inspect the work.

- As the building is finalized, many other inspectors will confirm compliance with zoning and other regulations.

- Lastly, the customer will review the work to confirm it complies with the agreed goals for their dream home – the ones agreed on in the first bullet point.

In this imaginary example, the architects, designers and builders are all – hopefully! – familiar with the backend tests, regulations, zoning requirements, and so on, that the code enforcement officials and inspectors will be using. Your job as project manager is to make sure that at the beginning of the project, the architects and builders know to perform their work in such a way as to ensure that all backend tests will be passed.

Despite the oversimplifications in the above example, the general point remains: today, designing and building a house has many knowledge worker components that settlers building log cabins didn't have to consider. The project involves both physical construction *and* knowledge work. Thus, even though the initial assumption might be that the end goal is a physical building, and therefore the waterfall model is the best place to start, we can see that the V-model lifecycle has a place in developing one's approach to managing such projects. This is true for many other fields – it's always worth checking your initial assumptions.

## The V-model/lifecycle philosophy

To recap, this model:

- is one approach to managing projects that involve some degree of knowledge work (as opposed to simple construction work);
- starts by considering how to test the success of our project;
- uses a hierarchical approach to designing our solution;
- links each step in our hierarchical design to a testing phase;
- enables us, if the testing at one stage identifies an issue, to go back a step and try again, until we pass the testing for that stage. (Plan for these iterations.)

# The rapid prototyping lifecycle

Once you have a prototype, the project is half way to success! Or so this approach to project lifecycle management goes.

## Michelangelo: an apocryphal story

I heard this story a long time ago. I cannot confirm its validity, but it is a great story nonetheless. The tale goes that early in Michelangelo's career, a wealthy client requested the installation of a piece of art on his property. After investing time and effort in creating the art, Michelangelo proudly finished the work. However, the client did not like the final product, and stiffed Michelangelo on payment. After that, Michelangelo learnt to develop prototypes, sketches and mock-ups first – and to get the client to approve the prototype *before* he would start work on the real creation. Often (so the story goes), Michelangelo would propose many versions before he could get approval. However, once all agreed on the prototype, success obviously followed, because now all Michelangelo had to do was implement the prototype. As a result, unlike many artists, Michelangelo died wealthy. (Unintended side effect of this policy: today, when people find a Michelangelo prototype, sketch or draft, it is often revered as much as the final products that we know and love. That is just how good Michelangelo was at his craft.)

Even if that story about Michelangelo is not entirely true, it makes some interesting points for knowledge workers: mainly, when creating something new, rarely will people get it right the first time. Yes, the first draft produced by talented, insightful, skilled people may be something wonderful (eg, Michelangelo's prototypes, sketches and drafts are wonderful pieces of art unto themselves). However, in business, doing something *good* is not good enough. What *is* good enough, what *is* the right answer, is doing what the client wants! In the story, Michelangelo kept producing 'drafts' and reviewing them with the client. Each subsequent draft took into account the feedback from the previous draft. The process was repeated, until all agreed. Once everyone agreed on the prototype, then one just had to implement the prototype to be successful; or so the theory behind this model goes.

Art may be the ultimate form of knowledge work. The artist creates the art completely from their ideas. Judgement of art is completely subjective. Similarly, a project may be creating something based entirely on the ideas of one or a few people. The client, customer or market may subjectively judge the results. The definition of success for many projects is in the eye of the customer – just like the success of art is in the eye of the beholder. So, then: anytime you find yourself managing a project that has a highly subjective component, or where it is impossible to nail down the requirements, or creating something completely new, you should consider using the prototyping model for defining your project.

## A prototype is an experiment

Why do scientists conduct experiments? It is to test a hypothesis, an idea or a theory. If you know with certainty the outcome, then it is not an experiment, it is a demonstration. The results of the experiment can give you information and insights that you did not previously have. The same is true of prototypes.

A cliché goes: 'Prototype as if you are right, then listen as if you are wrong.' This cliché persists in project management culture, because it captures an important perspective for a successful prototyping process. Specifically:

1   Do not be timid about prototyping. Of course, be cost effective, keep it on a small scale, and so on. But, make certain it represents all the things that you think are important to achieving success with the customer, or all the features that are important to your design, and so on.

2   When presenting your prototype to the customer, or when testing the features of your prototype, listen and look carefully for all the places where you are wrong. Being defensive at this stage, justifying why you are right, or trying to make it work, is the worst thing you could do. You are about to receive the most important information you will need to know for making your project a success. Do not waste this opportunity!

In one sentence, a prototype is an experiment where you discover how your theories are wrong, while it is still cheap and easy to become right!

## Spiral and RAD

According to his classic book, *Out of the Crisis*, W Edwards Deming (Deming, 1986) claims that in 1950, he introduced Japan to an idea published in 1936 by Walter Shewhart. Deming called this idea the Shewhart Cycle. In Japan they called it the Deming

Cycle, and the name stuck. Nowadays, many texts call this idea PDCA, or OPDCA – and might only trace its roots back to Toyota Production Systems. Regardless, this idea has become a fundamental tool for quality practices. Merge PDCA with ideas on prototyping, and you can re-derive the spiral and RAD lifecycle principles of project management.

We will begin by looking at Figure 7.8.

**Figure 7.8**    PDCA/OPDCA philosophy for the prototyping project management lifecycle

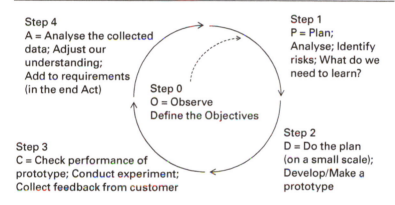

Step 4
A = Analyse the collected data; Adjust our understanding; Add to requirements (in the end Act)

Step 1
P = Plan; Analyse; Identify risks; What do we need to learn?

Step 0
O = Observe
Define the Objectives

Step 3
C = Check performance of prototype; Conduct experiment; Collect feedback from customer

Step 2
D = Do the plan (on a small scale); Develop/Make a prototype

5. (1b) Repeat step 1 with the refined understanding
6. (2b) Repeat step 2 with the new risk perspective from the repeated step 1
7. (3b), 8. (4b), 9. (1c) and so on until all are in agreement; then Act!

- Step 0: O is for Observe the current situation. Define the initial version of our Objectives for our project. What is the situation that is the motivation for this project? We call this Step 0 (zero) because we do this before we get started.

- Step 1: P is for Plan. In this step, we analyse and identify risks our project might face. Taking a scientific view, we ask: What do we need to learn so that our project can be successful? We develop a plan for learning that information, which may include building a prototype. A prototype may not be fully functioning. It simply needs to demonstrate the components under study so that we can answer the questions at hand.

- Step 2: D is for Do. Here we do the plan. The preference is that we do the plan on a small scale. We could also think of D as being for Develop (or make) the prototype, as needed to address the questions we raised in Step 1.

- Step 3: C is for Check the performance of the prototype. Conduct the experiment that our prototype embodies, or in other words, Collect the data and feedback generated from Step 2.

- Step 4: A is for Analyse the collected data. Adjust our understanding of what we must accomplish for this project to be a success. Add to our understanding of the requirements.

- Step 5 (1b): With these refined insights, we return to Step 1. This time we will call it Step 1b. Here we analyse and identify the risks our project might face, based on what we learnt from the previous prototype experiment. With this perspective, we refine our key questions, and develop a new plan.

- Step 6 (2b): Develop a new prototype.

- Step 7 (3b): Check the performance of the new prototype, collect feedback.

- Step 8 (4b): Analyse, adjust, add to our requirements.

and continue.

With enough spins through this cycle, we reach an understanding of what will make this project a success! We just have to implement the ideas represented by this version of the prototype. Let's call this Step 4y. Now, we move to Step 1z. Step 1z becomes a plan for implementation. Step 2z becomes developing the final plans for the final version of the product. Step 3z becomes construct/build/manufacture our product. And Step 4z becomes act: release, announce, ship… and enjoy/observe the successful acceptance by the customer! (Which sets you up for the next project.)

Why is this called the spiral model? Since the latter steps build on the former, the depiction of this process is often drawn as a spiral circling outwards until everyone agrees on the final version of the design.

**Figure 7.9** PDCA/OPDCA philosophy shown as a spiral lifecycle

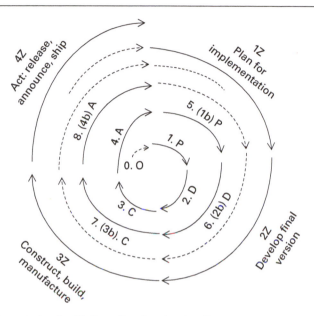

5. (1b) Repeat step 1 with the refined understanding
6. (2b) Repeat step 2 with the new risk perspective from the repeated step 1
7. (3b), 8.(4b), 9. (1c) and so on until all are in agreement; then Act!

RAD stands for Rapid Application Development. In short, one approach of RAD is to develop a series of prototypes, following something like that outline above. Each new prototype becomes successively more refined. Eventually (sometimes in software) the final prototype can become the product. With that we declare success!

As a result, even though when we started, no one had a clear understanding of the specifications for this product, by the time we get to the end of the process, we have come to a version of the product that we know will satisfy the customer.

# The Agile concept

In all our preceding project management lifecycles, the underlying assumption is that the order in which we do things is important.

The activities are context sensitive (ie, the activity only has its value if done after something else, and before some other thing). Suppose order did not matter? Then we could develop dramatically different models of project management.

Consider a team writing chapters for a textbook. The order in which the reader studies each chapter might matter. Let's say chapter 5 builds on concepts in chapter 4. So long as we know that when chapter 4 is written, it will cover those topics, then chapter 5 could be written before chapter 4 is written. Once we establish the framework of what needs to be in each chapter, the writing of the chapters is order independent. In such cases, a team of people can write the textbook by working on chapters independently of what other members of the team are doing. The team could self-organize how they get the work done.

Also, in our previous models, we consider requirements to be a fixed thing. Even if not fully documented at the beginning of the project, the idea is that requirements are a fixed concept our team just needs to discover.

Suppose one was working in an environment where the broad vision of what we are trying to achieve is known, but details about that goal are subject to change. This is not as uncommon as you might imagine; some projects may start with only a partial understanding of requirements, because the full understanding of the requirements cannot be known until we get a bit more into the project. Things we do in the project itself will help us determine what the requirements need to be. In such situations, it is possible that requirements might even change.

For circumstances like those described above, we need a different approach to managing projects.

## The new new product development approach

In January 1986 Hirotaka Takeuchi and Ikujiro Nonaka published an article in *Harvard Business Review*, titled 'The New New Product Development Game' (Takeuchi and Nonaka, 1886). They noticed that many new software development projects used approaches that did not fit classic project management lifecycles. They likened these approaches to the scrum of a rugby game. Everyone has their favourite components of this article (so don't be limited by my highlights); I happen to like the concepts of self-organizing teams, overlapping development phases, an acknowledgement of team rhythms, managing mistakes early before they are too expensive, and things like that. This article is a classic in the history of Agile. It is worth a read.

Supposedly, when Jeff Sutherland, Ken Schwaber and Mike Beedle read that article, it resonated with them. They expanded on the ideas, including the metaphor. They called their framework (or project lifecycle model) a Scrum framework. As of this writing, Ken Schwaber and Jeff Sutherland maintain a free download of their Scrum Guide at a brand-neutral site: www.scrum.org/resources/scrum-guide

But Scrum is not the only framework to address the above outlined challenges. On 11–13 February 2001, in Snowbird, Utah, a group of people who were thinking about these problems met for some skiing and discussions about software development practices. They came up with the Manifesto for Agile Software Development (see agilemanifesto.org for more details). This manifesto is comprised of four values and twelve principles. I encourage you to have a look for yourself.

By this point you might be wondering: when are we getting to the Agile method/lifecycle? The punchline of this section is that *Agile is not a method*. It's not a model, but an approach – a collection of principles and values, like those outlined in the manifesto referenced above. Some models or systems that attempt to embody the Agile values and principles are:

- Scrum.
- Crystal.
- Extreme programming (XP).
- Feature-driven development (FDD).
- Dynamic systems development method (DSDM).

There are many others. This list is not complete. I assume other Agile practices will be developed over time. Each of these methods has its strengths. It is far beyond the scope of this book to survey them.

## When should I be thinking Agile?

Agile is a philosophy that came from a small-group environment. It was implicit that people had close working relationships, with face-to-face communications. An additional characteristic is that progress came from short-term, iterative, incremental efforts. Workers could repeat things until they got them right. Additionally, the teams could self-organize what components of work were done when. One of the key features of the Scrum approach, for example, is that a backlog of tasks needing work is always available. The team can choose which tasks to work on during a 'sprint' of work. Finally, if there is a high degree of uncertainty around how requirements will be met (and requirements may be refined as we go) – your project might be suited to the concepts of the Agile manifesto, or one of the many practices or frameworks that support these values and principles.

### The Agile caveat

Look at the characteristics of the last section, and think about projects that do not fit. Ponder a project using a large, globally distributed, impersonal team. Consider that they must work on issues that take long periods to resolve. Imagine that the project is construction-like, where the order of activities matters. And just for additional fun, let's imagine that 'management' will say the requirements are flexible, as a way of facilitating their desire for scope creep – or simply as a way of avoiding the work (or political capital) it will take to get everyone to buy in to an explicit set of requirements. The sponsors of this project want to seem as if they are using the best methods, so they place a job posting for a project manager who is adept at applying 'The Agile Method' (which now you know is a dumb statement – because there is no such thing as 'The Agile Method').

I have seen many such situations.

Those who inappropriately pursue 'Agile' for the wrong type of projects are giving this valuable philosophy a bad name. Agile has appropriate uses; if one applies these values and principles to the right problems, in the right environments, with the right type of teams, then Agile thinking can be helpful. But it's not a magic wand applicable to every situation!

# The blended lifecycle – reality

Project management lifecycles, theoretical models, values and principles are great for books. In books, the author can create idealized settings, in which everything works out nicely. The real world is not idealized. With enough force and energy, it is possible to make almost any of these lifecycles work, in almost any situation. There is another way. I call this the blended lifecycle.

Projects of almost any substantive size and complexity will almost certainly not fit easily into any one of the lifecycles we just reviewed.

For example: consider planning a family holiday. Let's pick the waterfall lifecycle to create the perfect plan for the family holiday – it should be simple enough, right? First, you collect the **requirements** of what everyone will want to accomplish on the holiday. Then you **design** your trip so that all the requirements are met. Then you **implement** that design – you go on your trip. Along the way, **verify** that everyone is enjoying themselves as you tick off the list of requirements and goals. On return, consider what **maintenance** activities are needed, so that everyone can get back to life's normal routine.

That seems to fit perfectly!

The reality of our family holiday planning follows a slightly different lifecycle:

- Early on, videos of possible destinations are exchanged, pamphlets shared and proposed schedules floated, along with a sample budget (we do not have infinite money). The process is similar to **rapid prototyping**.

- Once we have settled on a general destination, a high-level **waterfall model** might be used for general travel plans, hotels, scheduling details, and so on.

- Then our waterfall starts backing up... maybe scrum-like teams develop around certain components: luggage packing, development of a dog management plan, and what about that fish tank? The whole family scrambles together, grabbing different tasks, in a particularly **Agile** fashion.

You get the idea!

In real life, different parts of a project are like different mini-projects unto themselves. To make each sub-part of the project work, you may use the approach that resonates with the team and the type of problem they are addressing. The successful project manager will use *all* the tools they have at their disposal.

If the technique is not helping – modify it so it does help. If part of the project does not fit the overall lifecycle approach you are using, then use a different lifecycle model or philosophy for that portion of the project. In my experience, the blended approach – one that uses all these methods appropriately, in their proper turn – is the most powerful lifecycle model.

## Summary points

- Projects are temporary creatures with lifecycles.

- There are many different frameworks and philosophies for organizing and managing the life of a project.

- Depending on the type of project at hand, you will find that one type of framework or philosophy may be more effective than other frameworks or philosophies.

- We looked at four frameworks (or models, or concepts, or philosophies) common in project management:

  - The waterfall lifecycle (or predictive method).

  - The V-model.

  - Rapid prototyping (RAD)/spiral approach.

  - The Agile concept.

- In real life, the blended approach will help the project manager gain the best chance for success: each portion of a project may be like a mini-project unto itself, requiring the project manager to use the appropriate framework, concept or philosophy for that portion of the project.

# *References*

Covey, S R (1989) *The Seven Habits of Highly Effective People: Restoring the character ethic*, Simon & Schuster, New York

Deming, W E (1986) *Out of the Crisis*, MIT Center for Advanced Engineering Study, Cambridge, MA

PMI (2014) *Requirements Management: Core competency for project and program success*, Project Management Institute, Inc, Newtown Square, PA

Takeuchi, H and Nonaka, I (1986) The new new product development game, *Harvard Business Review*, **64** (1), 137–46

# 08
# Planning the project
## Schedule management (time management)

*A goal without a plan is just a wish.*

ANTOINE DE SAINT-EXUPÉRY

Remember the opening scenario in Chapter 2? Did you notice there is no real plan for achieving the goal? Sure, goal setting is important, and can be motivational. Any project goal (and all project aspects) can seem feasible while plans are vague, or if it is someone else's job. But without realistic plans for achieving the goal, it's not really a goal; it is just a wish. This book is not about being successful through creative wishing. We are looking at how to be successful through better project management. This chapter is about developing and managing the schedule of activities that makes goals more than just wishes – that makes goals possible.

> **When doing additional research on this topic:** You will find two terms for the exact same thing. Prior to 2017, the industry term for this material was project time management. Suffice to say, this phrase led to some confusion. In 2017, with the 6th Edition of the Project Management Institute's *Guide to the Project Management Body of Knowledge* (the accepted industry standards), the term for this topic became project schedule

management. We will use the most up-to-date (and arguably most accurate) term; but when doing your own research, be aware of the previous name for this material.

The classic role of a project manager is that of activity planning and schedule management – what to do, and when it needs to be done. There are five core things essential to this role:

- The project manager must **define the activities** needed to reach the goal.

- Part of defining the activities will be **estimating the duration of the activities**.

- Some activities may have prerequisites/successor dependencies. Identifying dependency-based **sequences of activities** is important.

- Then there is the **schedule development** (some will consider this part of the previous bullet; we'll look at the subtle differences later on).

- And of course, the project manager must **manage the schedule**.

Feel free to add to this list. However, we will focus on these core components.

# What is an activity?

A dictionary will not give you the type of definition we need. We need a definition for an activity that will drive our project planning functions. Over the years, I have settled on a working definition for a valid project 'activity' that is based on a technical concept called IDEF0.

## IDEF0/IDEFØ

IDEF0 is a compound acronym that stands for **ICAM DEF**inition of Function Modeling, where Function Modeling is represented by the 0 or Ø (and ICAM stands for Integrated Computer Aided

Manufacturing). It can also stand for **I**ntegration **DEF**inition for Function Modeling. The concept was developed in the 1970s by the US Airforce to improve manufacturing productivity. For more details, you can see Draft Federal Information Processing Standards Publication 183 (1993), Integration Definition for Function Modeling (IDEF0).

Building on the concepts of IDEF0, I find that a valid project activity must have five features:

**Figure 8.1**   IDEF0-like definition of an activity

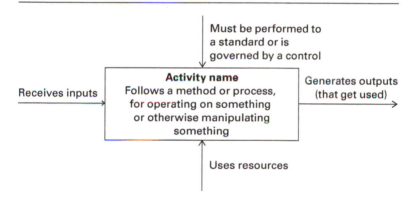

- Every activity receives **inputs** from someplace: our requirements documents might be the inputs, the outputs of previous processes might be the inputs, and so on. There is always an input.

- Every activity uses **resources**. It takes something to make an activity happen. Someone must be assigned to do it, and/or something is either used or consumed in the doing of the activity (we develop this component more in Chapters 9 and 12).

- The activity must be performed to a **standard**. It must comply with a specification of some type, or it is governed by some type of control. If there is no standard, specification or control, then there is no meaningful substance to the activity – anything is acceptable. If anything is acceptable, then don't waste time doing it. If it's not worth doing well (ie, to a standard), it's probably not worth doing.

- Using the preceding three things, a method or **process** is followed for operating on or otherwise manipulating, or transforming, something. If there is no method or process then there is no activity.

- Lastly, an activity must generate an **output** or a result that is used in some way. A number of years ago, I added to my definition that last bit about the output 'being used'. It may sound obvious, but I had run across a number of incidents where people were doing things that met all the other criteria for a project activity, but the outputs were not getting used in any way whatsoever. If in developing your project plan (or when taking over an existing project), you find activities that do not generate outputs, or the outputs are not used, you might have an opportunity for instant savings. If you delete such an activity, its absence has no negative impact on your project, because the output was not getting used. Not doing the activity can't hurt anything.

In my experience, every valid activity in a project that has to be performed must have these five characteristics – otherwise it's not valid. Sometimes these components are not obvious; but if your project has 'activities' where you cannot identify these things, then you may have a problem on your hands.

## Sequencing the activities

As noted in Chapter 7, some activities are context sensitive. The activity may have prerequisite needs (dependencies), and this activity could be the prerequisite for some subsequent activities (called successors).

A unit of sequenced activities might be grouped together into a 'summary activity'. This way, for discussion purposes, manipulation purposes, and so on, such a block of activities may be managed as one unit, despite the detail found within.

It is worth noting, however, that summary activities don't always mean a sequence of dependent activities. Sometimes parallel components or activities might be rolled up into a summary activity. In this way, a summary activity can be like a mini-project unto itself – see the box for an example.

---

### Paint the house: sequential and parallel summary activities

Consider that one is renovating a house. The project plan for the renovation might include a summary activity called 'Paint the house'. Within that activity, we might find sequenced activities like:

Sand/prep surfaces → prime → paint

These activities must happen in that order.

However, the sanding can happen while we are picking out the colour and brand for our paint. We must settle on the brand of paint prior to the priming activity, to ensure paint compatibility with the primer. The brand of paint and the colour selection activities may happen in parallel, but complete together. While there is some relationship between all these activities, the order of them is not necessarily sequential; some of the activities can happen at the same time. Yet, because they are all closely related, we might choose to summarize them all by a summary activity called 'Paint the house'.

---

So, we have our activities. We have identified dependencies and developed appropriate sequencing for such activities. We have grouped related activities into summary activities, knowing that some things within a summary activity may be occurring in parallel.

Now we have to order the summary activities. At a high level, we might manage summary activities as if they were simple activities – summary activities might have sequencing requirements or dependencies between other summary activities. From our house renovation project example, maybe we also want to 'Install new windows' and 'Refinish the driveway'. We might choose to 'Install new windows' first, in case that activity damages the exterior siding – because any damage could be repaired during 'Paint the house'. And maybe the summary activity for 'Refinishing the driveway' will be scheduled after 'Paint the house', just in case any paint gets spilled on the driveway.

# Estimating the durations of the activities

Now that we know what activities need doing, their dependencies, groupings and sequencing, we also need to know how long each activity will take to complete. This is a fundamental component on which all of project management relies. If you get everything else right, but you systematically underestimate the duration for the activities, your project will be behind schedule even before you get started.

Small problem: in general, as humans, we are not psychologically set up to process realistic estimates for how long things will take. Our brains tend to underestimate time and resource requirements. When confronted with the truth, in general, our brains cannot handle the truth.

## *The planning fallacy – people tend to underestimate*

Kahneman and Tversky (1977) did some groundbreaking research for DARPA (Defense Advanced Research Projects Agency) concerning military projects. Based on this research, they developed the **planning fallacy** – a description of the human tendency to chronically and consistently underestimate.

Classically, many components of project planning rely on intuitive judgements and educated guesses. The term *guesstimates* (often used synonymously for such estimates) implies that one is estimating something without having adequate information. In real life, plans must often move forward with incomplete information. We all make guesstimates. This is reasonable. Doesn't expertise and experience count for something?

Everyone can remember their good days, the times when their guesstimates were spot on. However, most people forget or subconsciously minimize their bad days. When scientifically tracked, Kahneman and Tversky found that when making project planning guesstimates, the experts are statistically no better than the non-experts. Other researchers have reproduced this result. Additionally, the research also shows that getting more opinions will not get you closer to the right answer – we can't correct this flaw by simply asking more people for their input. Why?

The bias most people have is to systematically minimize time and resource requirements. People tend to think things will take less time and require fewer resources than they actually will. Some think this is due to wishful thinking – but Kahneman and Tversky found that even when people would be penalized for underestimating (meaning the trend could not possibly be due to wishful thinking), they still tended to underestimate critical details. If *everyone* consistently underestimates, then even asking a huge range of people for their expert and experience-based guesstimates will still result in a net underestimation.

What is great about this understanding of Kahneman and Tversky's work is that it gives us a way to manage to it, which we will develop in a moment.

## Managing the planning illusion

Being aware of the planning fallacy, as a project manager, you will take steps to minimize its effects (as we will discuss below). For the moment, imagine you create an accurate plan and present that plan to upper management, who rightfully perceive themselves 'experts' in their business. Despite all your work, generally the first reaction of others will be to reject a realistic project schedule. Why?

Kahneman and Tversky also discovered that psychologically, planning errors are as insidious as optical illusions. Take your favourite optical illusion. Prove to yourself that it is an illusion (the thing your brain thinks it sees is not what is there). Then remove whatever allowed you to prove reality to yourself – and the illusion re-appears. The same thing happens when project managers share their planning results with others.

Others will tend to perceive that shorter activity durations and lower resource utilizations are possible. The project manager can prove why such perceptions are not true. Unfortunately, the 'experiences' others recall in their unaided minds tell them that the results of the project plan can't be right. You, of course, know why their unaided mind is failing them (because their recollections are not complete); but they cannot perceive what they are missing (otherwise they would not be missing it). Hence, despite any proof you muster, others will still feel in their gut that the project manager has overestimated things.

So what is the solution?

This problem is widely recognized. Yet no one has the universally accepted solution. If you find a solution that works for you, run with it. I like to use the following multi-pronged approach.

## Set the ground rules

When setting up the governance team (see Chapter 4), some rules must address project estimating. Namely, everyone acknowledges that estimates will seem too high (durations too long, resources too consuming, and costs will seem too expensive). If there are errors in the process that got you to these results, then we fix those errors *in the process*. We don't simply adjust the results. If the process is correct, then we all agree to accept the results of the process. We will not arbitrarily force our project to align with wishes.

## Small chunks and regular check-ups

I try to break activities into what I call 'activity atoms' and then build summary activities from them. The idea is to find small enough units of work that people can accurately know what it will take to perform it, without it being so small that unnecessary over-head develops from trying to manage it. In my experience, activity units of about two to three weeks long seem to work well. In Scrum (Agile), the accepted practice is that a 'sprint' (the time a team focuses on an activity) should range from about one to four weeks. This is consistent with my experiences for planning in general – but this can also be affected by the check-in/meeting schedule.

In the Scrum (Agile) approach, teams may have daily Scrum meetings. That works for them, because of the dynamic nature of the problems they are managing, and how a Scrum team functions. In other environments, daily project meetings might be too fre-quent; you do not want people to spend all their time in meetings – they need some time doing actual work.

In many environments, weekly meetings are the norm. A guide-line is that when weekly meetings are the norm, the shortest activ-ity atom a project manager can reasonably manage is about two weeks (and three- or four-week activities may be more appropri-ate). When people try to estimate activities that are more than four to six weeks long, I see the Kahneman and Tversky planning fal-lacy effects become dramatically pronounced – because the more an activity covers, the harder it is to remember everything that goes into it. So, when someone tells me something will take them six weeks or longer to do, I try to break that activity into meaningful 'atoms' that are two, three or four weeks long. Then, by building a summary activity, we reconstruct the estimate for the longer, over-all activity.

## Use real data

Whenever possible, relate the current activities being estimated to an experience for which you have historical data. Ideally, that data tells you how long the similar activity actually took, along with any caveats. Be advised: if historical data for an activity atom is longer than four to six weeks – it may be missing something.

## Check with the actual team

Confirm the activity duration estimates with the people who will actually be doing the work. It is best if you can get them to sign off and buy in to the estimates.

The process of actually having people sign off on anything has two effects:

**1** They are more likely to make certain their estimates are accurate before they sign off.

**2** Once they sign off, they are more likely to make the estimate work.

Cognitive dissonance theory tells us people do not like being wrong. They do not like having said *yes* to something and then acting differently. So, once they sign off on activity durations, they are more likely to do whatever they can to make what they said a reality. If the person doing the work was not forced into signing off on the activity duration, then cognitive dissonance helps you keep your project duration on target.

While getting sign-off from the people doing the work is a good thing, compare their past commitments to their past delivery performances. Most people will have a 'discount factor' that is consistent. If Frank tells you it would take him three weeks to get something done, but it typically takes him four weeks – then in the future add 33 per cent to all of Frank's estimates. If Kim told you something will take her four weeks to do, but she got it done in 4.5 weeks – then add 12.5 per cent to the future estimates that she gives you.

# A concluding word on estimating activity durations

Nothing ever ends at the exact time for which you schedule it to be completed. Estimating activity duration works better when given as a range. Many project management textbooks will tell you to track three points: the earliest possible time, the most-likely time, and the worst-case time. Unless you have a project planning software tool that manages that range for you, the three-point method quickly becomes impractical. Besides, the earliest possible time is typically unrealistic anyway, so why bother with it?

On the other hand, if you build your project schedule around the worst-case completion times, another psychological phenomenon can develop. For many, work expands to fill the time allotted to it. Even then, some people have a need to be just a little bit late, no matter how much time you give them.

My approach is to build a schedule around developed, or computed, activity durations. To get this number:

- I solicit input from the people who will be responsible and accountable for assuring the activity atom completes on time (as defined above). Get their most-likely guesstimate plus get a worst-case duration. Get them to sign off on each.

- I then add to both numbers any known discount factors to account for their past prediction performances.

- I take that result and average the discounted most-likely time with historical evidence. Whatever that effectively added to the most-likely guesstimate, add the same amount to the worst-case duration.

- The result is a computed most-likely time (MLT) and a computed worst-case longest time (WCT).

I now take the WCT and subtract the MLT, and this yields the difference for an activity (often called the 'delta' and represented by the Greek letter $\Delta$). So: $WCT - MLT = \Delta$

There are many philosophies and ways to think about how to use the 'deltas' in a project plan (some scheduling tools may allow you to enter this information and they will compute the impacts for you).

**Method 1** (the simple approach/split the difference): For all activities, find the WCT and the MLT, and then plan that activity using (WCT + MLT)/2. The idea is that the errors around $\Delta$ for each activity will average out in the course of the project. Some activities meet or beat the MLT, while others will meet the WCT. In a large project (in theory), it all balances out.

**Method 2:** As you build summary activities, plan things using the MLT, but collect the $\Delta$s for each activity. Then create a final activity – you could call it a wrap-up activity – that adds up all the time from all the deltas. Sometimes I will place this at the end of each summary activity, or sometimes just outside the summary activity. The governance team (and others) can then see that we are working to a 'stretch-goal' (it is going to be a stretch to make the MLT a reality, but that is our goal). However, when planning for things that rely on this project, we use the WCT (the result from appropriately adding back in the deltas). So, if we can close an activity quickly (we finish by the MLT), we take the win and move forward. Rarely will anyone be upset about a project completing ahead of schedule. But if needed, we have our $\Delta$-time available.

There are many other ideas on managing to this reality. Use what works for your environment.

---

### Warning
Watch out for *Wish-ti-plans* – plans based on wishes

Estimates are attempts to determine the value of something based on reason.

Guesstimates place value on something based on gut feelings (guesses, intuition, etc).

'Wishtimates' (a slang term used in some project management circles) place value on something based on a wish (what we want it to be, irrespective of anything else).

The type of project plan you have depends on the components that form the basis for that plan. Is it an estimated plan? A guess-ti-plan? Or a *wish-ti-plan*?

If the project manager knows from experience, or other fact-based sources, that an activity will take four weeks, but management *wishes* it to be done *this time* in two weeks, trouble is at hand. There are many ways in which components of a plan become wishtimates. Once done, no amount of intricate details or form of a project plan can give you a real project plan. It is now a wish-ti-plan: a plan based on wishes. This concept can apply to any facet of project planning – not just duration estimates. When in such a situation, one must develop a plan for managing the fall-out for when wishes are not realized.

# Scheduling the activities

With all the preceding information in hand, the activities need to be scheduled. Creating a good schedule is a bit like solving a multifaceted, dynamic puzzle. One must determine the start times for each activity. End times follow from duration information. So how is schedule development different from sequencing the activities – surely we did all of this in the previous stage? This is why many will roll those two stages together, but in my experience, activity sequencing is only *almost* project scheduling. The main difference is that in the previous stage we focus on the dependencies of the activities – but activities also use resources (remember our five features from the beginning of the chapter?). Are all the needed resources available when the activities will be happening? The schedule must accommodate all sequencing needs, including resource availabilities.

## Avoid the single thread

Real projects quickly become a complex web of activities, dependencies and connections. As we get into the details, the idealized lifecycles of Chapter 7 will evolve and grow to fit reality. The overall philosophies of the models remain important. For example: When will we be doing unit testing? What about user acceptance testing? Is there a portion of the project that will require prototyping? And so on. But, in a real project, if we only did one thing at a time, the overall duration of the project would take too long for anyone's liking.

When all the activities of a particular project, or sub-project or summary activity, occur in sequence, we call this a **single-threaded process plan**. Imagine a necklace made by sliding beads on to a single cotton thread. If that single thread breaks, all the beads fall off; the whole necklace is lost. The same is true of single-threaded process plans: if any step in the process fails or breaks, that failure jeopardizes timely completion of the overall process.

Consider the above two motivations: (1) that our project would take too long if we did all the activities sequentially; and (2) that single-threaded processes are potential failure points. This combination of motivations (and there are many more) becomes a strong impetus for developing a plan that takes opportunities to do things in parallel. Our project can become faster and more efficient, and also more resilient, by doing things in parallel; if something goes wrong with one part of the project, then you have the chance to recover that part without adversely impacting the project's overall delivery date.

Of course, rarely will you have sufficient resources to do *everything* at once. So even the execution of non-dependent activities needs to be scheduled, because they are dependent on resources.

## The critical path

An artefact that develops when constructing a schedule is something project managers call the **critical path**. To understand how project managers define and speak about the critical path, we first need to understand the jargon terms 'float' and 'free float'.

Imagine that you have a set of sequential activities, rolled up into a summary activity. Now imagine this summary activity is shorter than the overall duration of the project. Also, imagine that only *some* aspects of the final goal depend on this summary activity. So long as this set of activities completes before the end of the overall project, their completion has no impact on the delivery date. Thus, you could imagine these activities 'floating' around within your project plan; the scheduling of them is not at all critical, so long as they complete before the project's end. Project managers refer to this time between the end of these types of activities and the end of the project as the **float**. If you need to, you can delay starting a set of activities for an amount of time equal to their float, and you will not delay the completion date of the project. See Figure 8.2.

**Figure 8.2**   Depiction of float

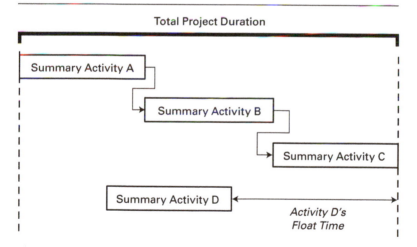

Now imagine that there is another activity that cannot start until our summary activity completes. The time between the end of our summary activity and the start of the dependent activity is called the **free float**.

With all that in hand, we can define the critical path for a project as anything that has zero float. This short definition has significant implications. Consider our set of single-threaded activities. If they have zero float, and no free float between activities, they become a critical path. Anything on the critical path is a **critical path activity**. If the completion of any critical path activity is delayed, the completion date of our project is delayed. (See Figure 8.3 – the bolded activities are a critical path.)

**Figure 8.3**   Depiction of free float and critical path

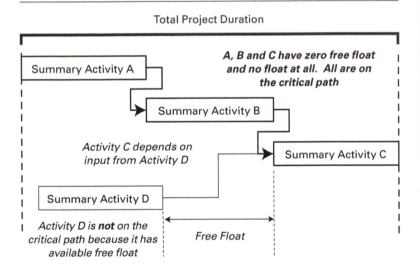

From a project scheduling perspective, project managers try to identify high-risk activities – things that are not likely to complete on time. Then they do everything possible to keep such activities off the critical path. Depending on how things slip, get moved, or re-planned, the critical path may change. Keeping an eye on the critical path, and making certain critical path activities execute smoothly, is typically one of the important things a project manager does to ensure success of their project.

> **Tip**
>
> The word 'slack' is often used synonymously with float. 'Total slack' is the total amount of time something can be delayed without delaying the end of the project. 'Free slack' equals free float.

# Managing the schedule

So: you have listed all the activities needed to achieve the project's goal, along with all their associated characteristics. You know all the dependencies and interrelationships needed to sequence the activities. You have worked out duration estimates that everyone agrees with. And, you have successfully created a schedule for the execution of the activities, accounting for resource needs. Everyone has bought into your schedule. You have woven together more things than you thought possible, to develop a schedule that not only seems feasible but also is artfully crafted. You sit back and think to yourself – this is good!

But, as the saying goes: no battle plan ever survives contact with the enemy. Execution, implementation and reality are the enemies of any project schedule. Collecting status updates, accommodating changes to resource availability, and re-planning for unforeseeable issues become major jobs for the project manager.

The tapestry of the project schedule you have created accounts for so many interrelated things that pulling on any one component will have ripple effects too numerous for you to imagine. The amount of work it will take to update your project schedule to accommodate changes can seem overwhelming.

Recall that in our definition for 'What is a project?' the theme was that the average person cannot manage some components of the effort without aid. It is time to have a serious discussion about tools.

## Project management tools

In general, this book emphasizes principles over technology. Principles tend to be long-lasting, whereas technology can be ephemeral. However, in project management, there is a point where current technology supports principles: this is where schedule management tools come in. As a project manager taking on the challenge of project schedule management, you will almost certainly need tools designed for this challenge.

I have seen modern, large organizations managing complex projects using nothing but spreadsheets. Such situations remind me that with enough manual labour, people can calculate, tabulate and file anything that a computer can calculate, tabulate or file. During the Second World War, rooms were filled with people who manually did complex numerical simulations for weapons trajectories and all sorts of things. Today, no serious business or military operation computes things via rooms filled with people doing sums; modern computing equipment with dedicated software is better for such challenges. Likewise, if you are going to be serious about managing a substantive project, in today's world, it is equally absurd to be using only spreadsheets or other manually intensive means.

If your PMO or organization does not have standard project management software, do some research. At the time of writing, there are many good project management software tools available at affordable rates; there are even some impressive public domain, freeware tools and web-based tools. Find something that fits your needs, that is affordable to your situation, and learn how to use it. Likewise, if your PMO or organization has standardized on a tool, learn how to use that tool. Then, you can focus on the concepts we discuss and not be hindered by the implementation aspects.

## Visualizations and common software features

Our brains are image processing wonders: stand too close to a Seurat pointillist painting and you cannot perceive the picture. But stand back and allow your brain to take it all in, and a Gestalt experience occurs – our brains find meaning in the underlying chaos of the visual image. We can see the Circus Sideshow (Parade de Cirque) that Seurat is depicting, or... we can see where problems or opportunities exist in our project plan. With a click of a button, modern software tools provide many types of visualization, at the desired level of aggregation or detail.

Your needs and preferences will vary, but the basic things I seek in project planning software are:

- **Gantt Chart functionality**: This is the classic horizontal bar chart that depicts activities against a timeline. You need to be able to excerpt sections of your project in this view. Also, you need to be able to aggregate or roll up sections of multiple activities into summary activities, in this view. In the Gantt Chart view, it becomes easy to see where activities can be done in parallel, where floats exist, and so on. Present-day project managers communicate by this *de facto* standard.

- **Interrelationships**: An ability to show dependencies, links and the relationships between activities (ie, which activities are prerequisites, successors, and so on). Typically, software will visualize this by drawing arrows connecting the bars of the Gantt Chart.

- **Critical path planning**: The software must be able to highlight the critical path. Really good project management software will help with re-planning and managing the critical path.

- **Automatic updates**: As you make changes to any of the activities (change the start date, duration, dependencies, etc), the software automatically calculates the impact to the schedule.

If your tool cannot do those four basic things, then I question if the software is useful as a serious project schedule management tool (which is why, in my opinion, a spreadsheet is not a serious project planning tool).

Figure 8.4 is an excerpt from a basic project scheduling tool, showing:

**Figure 8.4** Sample excerpt from a basic project scheduling tool

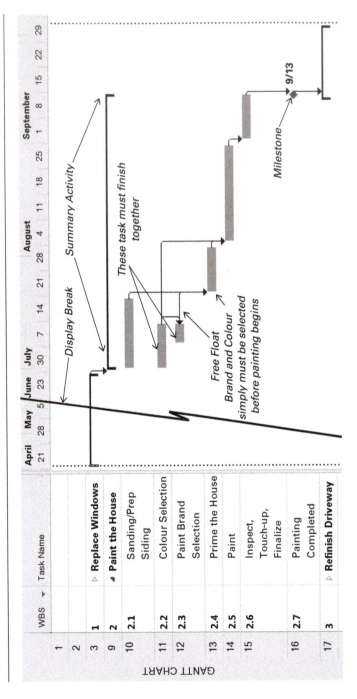

- activities displayed as a Gantt Chart;
- the dependencies between activities;
- where free float exists in the process;
- that activities can be summarized.

Additional useful features of this particular tool, not shown in the figure, include:

- Activities on the critical path can be highlighted in red.
- Links with slack/float time can be highlighted in colour for clarity.
- If any activity is adjusted, delayed, shortened, etc, the impacts to the dependently linked activities are updated automatically.

Other features that are helpful in a modern project scheduling tool:

- An ability to assign and manage resources associated with the activity. From this, most modern project scheduling tools can determine the loading of resources. If a resource is 'overbooked', the software will have various ways to visualize this. The tool will also give you ways to do load-levelling and rescheduling, so that resources are appropriately utilized.
- Depicting relationships to the work breakdown structure (WBS). Good project management software helps you visualize the relationship between the WBS → Activity → Resource assignment. Knowing everything in scope is covered by an activity, and the requirements for the people doing that activity, is key to project success (more on this in Chapter 9).

## Tracking progress, updating the schedule and re-planning

When it comes to tracking progress, updating the schedule and re-planning the project, this is where modern software tools shine.

Really good project scheduling software integrates information from other parts of the organization. Specifically, it will integrate with:

- other departments, allowing them to submit detailed plans for summary activities;
- time reporting tools, allowing people to book their time against various activities of the project schedule;
- progress reporting, allowing people to report on how much progress they have made on activities.

Before these tools existed in their current forms, a project manager needed to hold numerous meetings, hunt down people to collect information, and manually update the project plan to show how work was progressing against the plan. In small organizations, this may still be the most practical approach; and even in large organizations, personal follow-ups are often important. However, modern network- or cloud-based software can affordably deliver the most advanced features that were once only available to well-funded organizations with large IT support departments. If the organization, and project, is of any modest size, where even modest effort would be required to hunt down people for status updates, such tools can seem invaluable.

Without the right tools, maintaining an accurate perspective on project status, updating the plan and rescheduling becomes onerous. To facilitate these things, use the right tools (and get the organization to support the use of the right tools).

## Summary points

- Goals without plans are wishes.
- Beware of *wish-ti-plans*: things that look and act like real project plans, but have one or more components based on what people *wish* might happen, not what is realistically reasonable or possible.
- Activities have five defining features. If you cannot identify these five things, you probably do not have a handle on the

activity. An activity: receives inputs; uses resources; is performed to a standard or control; follows a method or process; and generates outputs that are used.

- Some activities need to be sequenced; they have predecessors or successors that are important to an activity's success.

- Activities take time to perform. Due to the planning fallacy, we cannot use intuition or even expert opinion to estimate how long something will take, so:

  - The governance team must support the estimating process.

  - Create activities that can be completed in two to four regular meetings. If meetings are weekly, an activity should be no longer than four weeks. If meetings are daily (as in some Agile projects) then an activity should be much shorter (as Agile activities tend to be).

  - Relate current activity durations to historical examples whenever possible.

  - Confirm duration times with, and get sign-off from, the people who will actually be performing the activity.

- Develop schedules that take into account most-likely durations, as well as worst-case durations.

- Activity scheduling must consider the use of resources.

- Always pay attention to a project's critical path, and keep high-risk activities off the critical path when possible.

- Learn about and use the software tool your PMO has selected as their standard. If your PMO has not selected a standard – find one appropriate for your purposes and learn how to use it.

## *Reference*

Kahneman, D and Tversky, A (1977) *Intuitive Prediction: Biases and corrective procedures*, Technical Report PTR-1042-77-6, Advanced Decision Technology, Defense Advanced Research Projects Agency, Office of Naval Research, United States

# 09
# The project staffing plan

There are a number of things that a project manager must consider as they develop their staffing plan:

- What type of labour is needed for the problem? And what skills must they have? Are labours properly qualified?
  - Commoditized labour (almost anyone can do the job – the worker is something of an interchangeable 'commodity').
  - Skilled labour (the person's ability or experience impacts their productivity).
  - Knowledge labour (the work turns on their thinking abilities, or knowledge of the field).
  - Expert labour (this work requires a specialist in the field).
- How can resource allocation change completion time of the task – will more people help get it done faster?
- What will it take to manage the assigned resources?
- Are any resources unique? (Is that the only person who can do the job?)
- Is there a back-up resource plan? (How will illness, injury or staff turnover be managed?)
- What will be the loading of the resources? Are people being overworked or underutilized?

(If there are other things your environment needs to consider, feel free to add to this list.)

Now that you know what a project's resource staffing plan needs to accomplish, how do we go about doing that?

First check in with your organization's Project Management Office (PMO) to see if they have some guidelines they want you to follow. Understand when and how your organization's HR (human resources) department needs to be involved – especially if you are hiring labour. Also, depending on the type of project manager you are, or the type of PMO your organization uses (see Chapter 3), your HR department may have additional duties for you to fulfil. If you are using temporary labour, outsourced labour, co-sourced labour or other forms of labour, the purchasing department may also have some input you need to consider. Understand your organization's expectations for your role and use any guidance they provide.

# Staffing

Most organizations use four typical sources for staffing projects:

1 In-house resources: These people already work for your company. Someone in the company is accountable for the management oversight of the resource. Typically, they are assigned to the activities of your project, as needed, by the person accountable for their management.

2 Customer-provided resources: These resources come from the customer's organization. The customer's organization manages these people. They will support certain project activities as needed. (If the customer recruits people or sources their activities to a third party, we still count that here, because the customer is managing it.)

3 Recruited resources: Your company may recruit people to work on this project. Once recruited, someone in-house will be managing their work (as in category 1 above). Typically, if your organization will be hiring people, HR handles much of these administrative details. However, if the people will be sourced

via an outside vendor, perhaps the purchasing department, or combination of purchasing and HR, might manage this type of recruiting.

4 Sourced or expert resources: Consider that your organization sources the activity to a third party, who will supply and manage the activity's resources, until the activity is closed. (Typically, someone administers these relationships. It could be the purchasing organization, HR, both, or a special administrator.) Sometimes such third parties might be in the form of experts or 'true consultants'.

---

### Tip

Sometimes, temporary workers may be referred to as 'consultants'. A true consultant *self-manages* their work, to create a final product (category 4). If the company manages the activities of the worker, they're probably not a consultant, but are temporary staff (category 3). There may be HR, legal and organizational implications to this distinction. Work with your PMO, HR, legal and governance team to avoid problems.

---

## Relationship management

In all these cases, someone else is responsible for the management oversight of the people performing the work. You as the project manager also have a degree of oversight, but unless you are part of a directive PMO (see Chapter 3), then most likely, you will not be the resource's manager. You may interact heavily with the resource, you may directly discuss the activities with them, directly monitor, organize, assign new tasks, cajole, herd… but in most cases, you are not actually the person's manager. Bear in mind that they will pay more attention to their manager than to you, because the manager is the one who (figuratively) signs their cheque, does their performance review, and is the person they have to live with after the project.

As with all things, real life may not be so clear. Even on the same project, there can be many different types of relationships between the project manager and the resources, depending on the source of the resources and even how their management wants to govern the relationship. As you staff the project, it is important to find out what the relationship will be between you and the people doing the work. Understanding that will help you know who you need to go to when acquiring resources, how you will manage the resources and what the scope of your responsibility and authority is, in terms of managing the resources.

All the nuances aside, generally you need buy-in and support from the managers of the resources. You need management's buy-in to secure the resource. You need their buy-in for assigning activities to the resource. You need their buy-in to prioritize the resource's attention. This is also true when it comes to hiring people; you need buy-in from HR. For sourcing relationships, you need buy-in from purchasing or the manager over that relationship. Depending on your organization and the nature of the project, you will need to get buy-in from many different people. Your governance team is typically a good source of guidance for these things.

As you review the tasks, you will begin to identify the types of resources you will need. Consider from where those resources will be coming. Identify the management of those resources. A representative of that management may need to have some role on the governance team – so that they can buy into and support the project, and in turn support you in supplying you with the resources needed to make this project happen.

By defining things this way, it effectively means that you will be going to the governance team for all your resources. This simplifies communications, presentations, meetings and interactions. With that said, the reason why I talk of resources in the four categories listed above is because even though conceptually you will be going to the governance team for all four types of resources, each type of resource source will have its own issues:

- In-house resources: You will need to manage internal politics and organizational trade-offs.

- Customer-provided resources: Whoever is responsible for managing this customer may need to handle various components of this.

- Recruited resources: Lead times for acquiring these resources, onboarding, and time to become effective must be considered (you may even build this into your project plan). Once recruited, you will need to work with whoever will be managing them.

- Sourced or expert resources: May have special availability limitations, access needs or other requirements. Handing a unit of work to a third party requires that you clearly define needed deliverables, requirements for deliverables and all other parameters for that work. This can become like a mini-project within the project.

Books have been written about managing various types of labour. I will not belabour the acquisition problem beyond this idea:

- Develop and staff your governance team so that it represents a full breadth of organizational experiences.

- Be aware of these issues.

- Then, work with your governance team to build your project team – while keeping an eye out for the various dynamics that accompany the different types of labour. Their experiences will help you do what is right for your organization.

## The back-up plan?

While staffing a project, keep in mind that these are people. They are not laser-hardened cogs or sprockets, engineered machines or robotic automatons. They are people. They are vulnerable to illness, injury and off-days. Also, their 'software' – the way they interpret, process and remember things, the way they approach and work with others – is not always easily predictable. Yet your project cannot happen without people-based resources. All projects depend on humans. At some level, all business is personal, because it all depends on *persons*. Never lose that perspective, or your project can quickly become troubled.

At the same time, you have an obligation to *all* the people on the project, to help them all succeed, and to the organization as a whole to help it be successful. Without lessening or diminishing in any way the importance of the individual, remember: the project is still the thing. To do what is right for all the individuals, it is important that no single problem with any single person destroy the success for everyone. It is important, then, to have a resource back-up plan – especially for resources on critical path activities.

The easiest problem to fix is the one you avoid. Here, I think, that begins with always remembering to appreciate the people working on your project, and appreciating that they are people. Then, in your staffing plan, consider: if they should become unavailable without warning, how will the project continue? Do we have a 'records plan' so we know the current state of their work at any given time? Can someone pick up their records and keep the job moving? Is someone being mentored by them? Cross-trained? Or, do I have someone else in the organization that can fill in for them? Is their back-up:

- hot (N+1 teaming);
- warm (generally familiar with the project and work – so they can readily pick it up); or
- cold (yes, I have someone that can do the job, but it will take them a while to *come up to speed*)?

# Defining the resource need – skill traceability

When staffing a position, managers often have trouble finding and hiring adequately qualified people. Typically, there are two reasons for this problem. The first is that what the hiring person is *really* saying is they cannot get a good person to work this job, *for what they are willing to pay.*

Several different people discovered the law of supply and demand. It is a *law* of free, competitive, capitalistic markets. Like physical laws, say the law of gravity, you cannot break the law; you can only break yourself against the law. Instead of breaking yourself against the law of supply and demand, use the properties of your environment to help you solve your problem. Simply put, all else being equal, if you are willing to pay enough, the law of supply and demand tells us the supply will become available. Anytime you can reduce a problem to price, you do not have a problem; you simply have an expense.

The second reason people have trouble getting 'good people' to fill a job is that the hiring manager has not properly defined what 'good' means. Most people are 'good' people. What the hiring manager really means is they need someone who can do the job properly. The hiring manager's problem is finding people who will do the job properly, up to expectations, meeting the demands of the job, and so on. To hire that person, the manager must first know what the **real** specifications are for the job.

At this point, you will have worked the project schedule to a level of detail such that you now know the activities your project needs to complete. To get these activities completed, you need to assign resources (ie, people or teams of people) to those activities.

Using the work breakdown structure (WBS) and/or the requirements traceability matrix (RTM), you can trace an activity back to the requirement(s) that an activity will be fulfilling. This is important, because most activities are context sensitive; the context in which they occur gives the activity part of its meaning. When specifying the skills and experiences a resource will need for the activity, looking at the activity alone tells only part of the story. The project requirements that the activity supports (found via the RTM) frame the skills needed for the job.

For example, suppose the activity is to have wait staff keep diners' glasses filled. The activity does not define the specifications for the job. If the 'project' requirement is to facilitate peak demand at a truck stop, this differs dramatically from a 'project' requirement to support a private, formal, catered dinner. The person who is successful at one of these activities may not be a good fit for the other and vice versa. If this is true for the simple task of filling diners' glasses, imagine how much more true this will be for the activities of your project.

Often, when you look at the context of the activity (ie, the project requirement that needs to be addressed), the requirement might imply the need for various certifications, industry familiarity, and so on. If you are in a regulated industry, you might have to show regulators the link from the requirement to the certification or proper training of the person working on that activity. Framing the activity in the context of the project's requirements is important to getting the job specifications right.

Also, do not overdo it. In Chapter 6, we discussed 'quality' as meeting the customer's requirements: no less and no more. In defining a person's skill set, we reverse the expression: when you can specify exactly what you need from someone, no less and no more, then you have a quality job description. Many people add qualifications that go beyond the needs of the task or job. They think this improves the quality of the resource. As noted in Chapter 6, going above and beyond, typically has the opposite effect. The same is true when asking for qualifications that are not applicable. I'll leave it to you to imagine all the possible ways needless job requirements can result in problems for the manager, the company as a whole, and the person that ends up in that over-specified position.

An activity is not just the activity. The requirements the activity addresses provide important contextual framing. As mentioned above, the requirements may imply needs for certifications, industry familiarity, and so on. Traceability between the requirement and the qualifications of the person doing the activity may be important. To get the right person – a quality resource, with the right experience – specify exactly what is needed, no less and no more.

# Schedule timing and resource loading

To gather your resources, you will be approaching your governance team. They will want to know when the resource is needed, and for how long it is needed. At this moment, assume you have developed the perfect project schedule. It details exactly what is needed, and when; and you have well-developed resource specifications. If you get the right resources and follow the plan, you see a win in your future. So far, all your work has been theoretical. Now begins reality.

Often the resources you need are not available when you need them, and you might have to rework your project schedule to fit the availability of resources. Re-developing a new schedule is usually no big deal; with the right tools (see Chapter 8), even a complex project can be effectively re-sorted.

Now, suppose the type of resource you want is not available at all. Instead, several people with different skills are available, in a timely fashion, at economical rates. Can you rework the project schedule so that a different set of tasks, using differently skilled people, can satisfy the same requirement? When this happens, the project manager takes on the role of project manager-*engineer*.

The reality of project management *after the planning* (if you will) is that a project manager must *surf* reality (a surfer does not control the waves, but works with the challenges they get to create a great ride – the same can be said of project managers). In the face of reality, the project manager must contrive a solution that still meets the project's requirements. Reality is imperfect. Resources are imperfect. Suppliers, components, timing, human nature, organizational dynamics... the list is endless, but rarely is anything perfect. Yet the goal, the requirements of the project, must still be achieved.

The project manager is not an industry-specific engineer; that is not necessary. Rather, the project manager will work with those skilled in the industry to rethink the plan (usually these people will be found on the governance team or through people on the governance team). The project manager then proposes a new plan, and uses the tools of their profession to see how these alternatives might come together to meet the requirements or goals of the project.

---

**Tip**

If someone proposes changes to the requirements, in order to make the project doable (which may be a perfectly reasonable thing), see the discussion in Chapter 5 on change control.

---

Additionally, the 'loading' of the resources is a concern. Bluntly, how much load can you put on any particular person? How much work can you expect from them on the needed days? Many scheduling tools might represent this as what percentage of the resource's time can be available to your project when you need them.

Often people believe that asking more and more from workers will get more output from the workers. If this were true, then much of management would simply be a quest to find new ways of motivating people. While this might work for a while, I have yet to see the case where, in the end, the organization as a whole does not eventually suffer detrimental effects from this type of thinking.

Fredrick Taylor's work should have settled this notion back in 1919. He demonstrated that there is even a 'science of shovelling' (Taylor, 1919: 65–70) that enables the best performance from a shoveller. One key component is that the load put on the shoveller can be optimized: too little load is unproductive, but also too much load is unproductive. Many have reproduced this finding across many different industries. Overload people in any aspect of life, and ultimately, over time, the return you get is less!

## Is time tracking unloaded or loaded?

How organizations account for people's time differs greatly.

1   Unload time-tracking accounts for work on the project separately from time on administrative or organizational activities. Thus, **100 per cent of the person's time is not available for project work**, because some of their time must be spent on administrative or organizational activities.

2   Loaded time means that the time they spend on the project must include administrative and organizational demands. Here, I often see people estimate what the task requires without considering organizational realities. To that they add 15 per cent to cover administrative overhead and such. There is nothing magical or absolute about that 15 per cent number. Each organization will have its own ideas on this. If your organization uses this method, find out what is their accepted practice.

Either way, people must still do all those other administrative and non-project things that come with being in an organization. If your project does not account for this reality, then your project will not be successful in reality.

Many project scheduling/project management tools (as discussed in Chapter 8) have the ability to re-adjust task durations, sort tasks, and do all sorts of nifty things so as to level the load. They will also be able to show you how your resources are being allocated, and flag resources that are being overloaded. Use the tools, and the support of your governance team, to *engineer* a plan that is feasible with the resources you have, without overloading them.

# Resource management

As you assign resources to activities, and the plan comes to life, you will need to manage the resources. In Chapter 13 we will talk about project execution, tracking reporting, and so on. How you collect data on what your resources are doing, how you keep them informed of overall progress, giving them their next assignments, and the like, will depend on the project environment, tools being used, nature of the work being done, and so on. We will not belabour these things, because they are unique to your environment. Still, consider the importance of establishing an infrastructure that supports:

- communication with the project resources;
- organizational identity of the project resources;
- teaming of the resources; and
- project focus of the resources.

Many will emphasize the tools, nifty tech, methods, and such, which facilitate these things. While all that is helpful, there is still something to be said for periodic group meetings, personal connections, and using the support of the governance team.

At some level, all of resource management comes down to applied human-engineering skills. We discussed this in Chapter 2. Now one must apply those skills. People are what make activities happen. To get an activity done, you need to get a person to do it. As project manager, you need to manage their efforts at getting the activity done.

By the way, just because you are managing the activities of a person, that does not make you the person's manager (unless that is how your organization defines things). Rather, you are there to coordinate, organize, inform, assign... and basically do what is necessary to get the human component to do the right thing at the right time for the benefit of the project.

Whole books are written about managing and organizing people. Even then, what works best in your organization may depend on the industry in which you are working, the overall cultural environment, and many other factors. Spend some time studying your industry around this point, and the literature in general. Through it all, keep in mind that behind all these systems there are people. Stay focused on helping them do their best. When you do that, I am confident that will be what is best for your project as well.

## Summary points

- Before you can develop a staffing plan, you need to know what type of staff you need: commoditized labour, skilled labour, knowledge labour, expert labour.

- Develop the governance team to support the sourcing strategy.

- Develop plans to manage resource problems – especially if the resource is on a critical path task.

- Show the connection between the resources doing an activity and the requirement supported by that activity. That requirement frames the specifications the resource must embody to succeed. It may also identify the need for certifications, training, and so on.

- To get the right person working on an activity, specify exactly what is needed; no less and no more.

- Understand the scheduling and loading of the resources. In the long run, overloaded resources produce less and are less effective on the project.

- When it comes to managing resources, start with a good infrastructure for connecting with the team. Build on that!

- Stay focused on helping your resources apply their best efforts to the project. When the resources succeed, that tends to help the project succeed.

## *Reference*

Taylor, F (1919) *The Principles of Scientific Management*, Harper & Brothers, New York

# 10
# Design and configuration management

The topic of configuration management (CM) can be a little abstract. Most dictionary-like definitions for this term seem to muddy understanding. To give you a feel for what this topic addresses, we'll start with a deadly serious example. From that, we will sort out the CM concepts that project managers need to consider.

## A deadly serious example

Imagine your project involves designing a set of hanging walkways for an upscale hotel. These walkways leave an open feel to the atrium space, because of their unique design. The design uses the concept seen in Figure 10.1.

Multiple walkways hang off the same rod, leaving the atrium view uncluttered by multiple supports. The top part of the rod must bear the combined weight of all the walkways below. Securing the rod to the roof will require some special means, but the engineers have a solution for that.

By hanging all the walkways off the same rod, each bolt on which the walkway rests only has to transfer the weight of that walkway on to the rod. This becomes a key feature of the design.

Anyone that has overtightened a screw or bolt to the point of stripping the threads knows that bolts or screws have a limited

**Figure 10.1**  Original configuration of hanging walkways

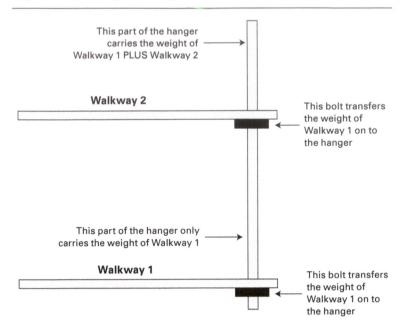

capacity for carrying loads. Bolts and brackets can be designed for carrying all sorts of loads, but typically, things that carry heavier loads cost more. This design can use less expensive parts and materials because each bracket only has to support the weight of its walkway – and the expensive fixture is used only once at the top to secure the rods to the roof.

On seeing this design, the construction company realizes that fabricating and working with these rods will be difficult. The rods need to extend all the way from the ceiling to the lowest level; they will be long. They will need to be threaded along the entire length of the rod. Such threads could be damaged during construction. Assembling this configuration will not be easy.

The construction company proposes a *minor* change that they think will make everything easier: use shorter rods, and hang the lower walkway from the walkway above it. This retains the desired

**Figure 10.2**   Configuration of hanging walkways that got built

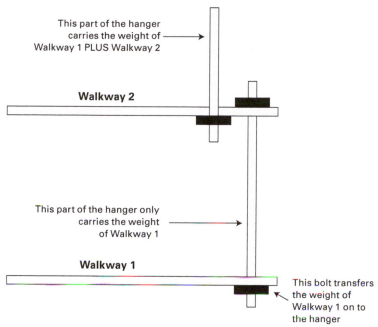

This part of the hanger carries the weight of Walkway 1 PLUS Walkway 2

Walkway 2

This part of the hanger only carries the weight of Walkway 1

Walkway 1

This bolt transfers the weight of Walkway 1 on to the hanger

open space requirement, because the rods will connect at the hanger for the upper walkway, so no one at a distance will be able to tell the difference. Figure 10.2 shows the configuration that got built.

Without a good CM system, it is frighteningly easy to talk a room full of bright engineers into this design change. The construction company changed a key feature without knowing it. Without a good CM system, there is no traceability to identify this key feature change, and the need for a detailed review.

A *key feature* of the design was that each bolt only supports the load of *one* walkway. When a CM-triggered review checks how much load the bolt holding Walkway 2 must now support, an analysis like Figure 10.3 results.

**Figure 10.3**  As-built configuration problem revealed

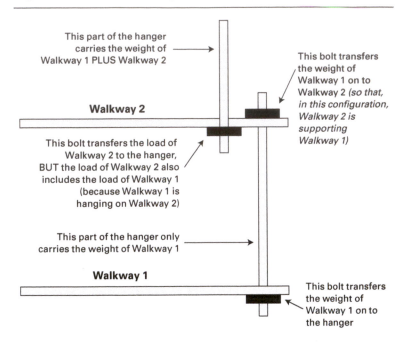

This part of the hanger carries the weight of Walkway 1 PLUS Walkway 2

This bolt transfers the weight of Walkway 1 on to Walkway 2 *(so that, in this configuration, Walkway 2 is supporting Walkway 1)*

**Walkway 2**

This bolt transfers the load of Walkway 2 to the hanger, BUT the load of Walkway 2 also includes the load of Walkway 1 (because Walkway 1 is hanging on Walkway 2)

This part of the hanger only carries the weight of Walkway 1

**Walkway 1**

This bolt transfers the weight of Walkway 1 on to the hanger

Once you change key features, you cannot consider the change to be an incremental adjustment to the old design. When key features of the configuration are changed, you effectively have a *new design.* The new design needs a new design review, and as project manager you need to make certain that happens. From the review seen in Figure 10.3, one quickly realizes the bolts or brackets supporting the upper walkway not only carry the load of its walkway, but also now carry the load of the walkway below it. Clearly, if you use the same bolts and brackets as previously specified, even a casual observer can see that failure will soon follow.

One goal of CM systems is to identify where changes impact designs, so designers find issues before they become problems.

The above example is an oversimplification of the issue that led to a catastrophe on 17 July 1981 at the Kansas City, Missouri, Hyatt Regency hotel:

On July 17, 1981, at approximately 7:05 p.m., two suspended walkways within the atrium area of the Hyatt Regency Hotel in Kansas City, Mo., collapsed, killing 111 people and injuring 188. Two of the injured subsequently died. In terms of loss of life and injuries, this was the most devastating structural collapse ever to take place in the United States [up to that point, *comment added*]. (Marshal *et al*, 1982)

Keep in mind, the project manager is *not* supposed to be a great engineer, programmer, chemist, and so on; they are *not* an expert in that field. Rather, the project manager manages the processes of the project to enable the expertise of those *working* on the project to shine.

Had a good CM system been in place, it is reasonable to assume that when the change to the walkway configuration was proposed, the change control process would have shown that it was modifying key features of the configuration. At that point, the project manager would have requested a full analysis of the new configuration. When the new loading analysis was done, the problem caused by this new configuration would have been recognized. Disaster would have been averted. Lives would have been saved.

# So who is responsible for managing configuration management?

From the opening example, we can see that CM is a **shared responsibility**. Both the project manager and the design team working on the project must team up to make CM work. Requirements, changes to requirements, and anything else that needs approval from the governance team are clearly things the project manager needs to manage. How requirements *manifest* themselves in the widget our project is creating is clearly in the design team's purview. As such, the project manager needs to make certain the design team is appropriately involved in reviewing changes to the design (especially when key features change, or when changes impact key features).

Project managers (no matter how experienced they are with a field) must avoid the tendencies to think they understand the impact of a change (no matter how minor – especially if a key feature is involved). Once a key feature is touched, get the design team/design engineers involved.

Each industry will have its own tools, methods, practices, and approaches for addressing not only the interface between the project manager and the design team, but also for handling CM issues. As with everything else in project management, your best resource for figuring out how your organization addresses CM issues will be your organization's PMO. Absent that, work with your governance team and design team to develop ways that work best for your organization and your project. If you are establishing a CM system for your organization, or seeking to improve your organization's CM system, you will need to do further research.

# Formally defining configuration management

For our purposes, we define 'configuration' of a widget (the project's output) as the description of how the components of the widget are arranged or set up; how they interact or otherwise work to satisfy the requirements; and it may also include the processes by which those components are brought together, and the resources used for doing so.

We assume our widget has some complexity to it, otherwise a project would not be needed for creating it. When changes are proposed to the configuration of the widget, a number of inherent problems develop. The simplest problem of CM is version control. Then (as in our opening example), how do you understand the impacts of changes to something that is complex? Both of these problems are addressable by the same solution: a good CM system.

## Configuration management for changing a thing

Assume we have successfully developed version 2.0 of the widget. Version 1.0 and Version 2.0 both serve the same purpose, but 2.0 is a bit more reliable, easier to make, cheaper and faster.

How version 2.0 implements the key features will differ from how version 1.0 implemented those features. When one works on different versions of the widget, orders spare parts or uses the widget in different environments – how will you know what components of the widget apply to the problem at hand? Which spare parts to order? What environmental conditions apply to this version? A good CM system will allow you to answer these types of question by tracking your version of the widget back to the relevant supporting 'configuration artefacts' (the things that define the widget's configuration).

## Configuration management for the impacts of change

At the other end of the spectrum, when a change is proposed to something complex, it is important to know what the cascading impacts of that change will be. When a change is made to a component of your widget, how do you trace the impact that change will have on the widget's features? Or suppose a requirements change is proposed: how do you discover all the things that need to be changed to meet that new requirement? A good CM system helps you understand how all of the different factors interplay, so that changes can be made without unintentionally causing disaster elsewhere in the configuration web that defines your widget.

With these as our goals – knowing what to do, and knowing how to manage the impact of what we're doing – we develop our CM system.

# Configuration management and project requirements

Configuration management is the management of the elements of your project's output, how they interact and fit together, and (sometimes) the process by which these elements are brought together for the final output. That last part of the definition is important, because in some industries, the process *is* the product. For example, software may have certain operating system requirements; or in pharmaceuticals, bringing two chemicals together in the wrong way will change what final product you create.

Now consider the project requirements for a moment. Generally, they cover all the requirements for the project. This means that the requirements document will contain requirements about the goals of the project, resource constraints, deadlines, and so on – and it *may* also contain requirements about characteristics of the widget our project will produce.

As we talk about CM issues, project managers often bifurcate requirements into non-functional requirements and functional requirements. Functional requirements specify the characteristics that the widget is to embody, while non-functional requirements are everything else. Often the point of a project may be to define and design the widget. Thus, in some projects, functional requirements can result from the designer's efforts to meet non-functional requirements.

Figure 10.4 depicts the relationship between these concepts.

In reviewing Figure 10.4, we see that the project requirements (and change requests) drive the project activities. Some of the project activities may determine additional widget design requirements or characteristics. As the project defines and designs the widget, the project will be producing documents, databases, plans – *whatever is needed* – to describe the creation of the project's widget. Each industry and business may have its own list of things that meet these criteria. These things – or artefacts – collectively define the widget's configuration.

**Figure 10.4** Conceptually where configuration fits in the overall project

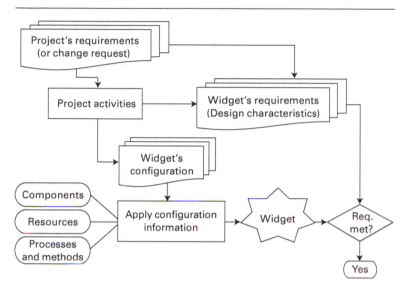

When one applies the widget's configuration to components, resources, processes, methods, and so on, the widget is created. If you have the widget's configuration information, you can create that widget.

Of course, we compare the created widget to the widget's requirements. Assuming the widget meets the requirements, we have been successful. If the widget does not comply with the requirements, of course we continue working project activities and revising the widget's configuration until we create a successful widget.

This implies that even without change requests, design changes can happen, giving rise to a need for a **traceable** version control over the configuration information. **Traceability is important**: you need to know which version of the configuration has which problems with meeting the requirements. As the team proposes a new configuration design, it is important to link the reason for this new version of configuration information to how it is addressing those issues. This will help later developers understand why things are done the way they are being done.

For practical purposes, the design characteristics are also part of the CM system. Since some of the design characteristics may have come from the project's requirements (or change requests), the 'functional' components of the overall project requirements (and change requests that impact key characteristics of the widget) may also fall under the control of the CM system.

Figure 10.5 highlights the concepts that comprise what the CM system may need to control.

**Figure 10.5**    What configuration management controls

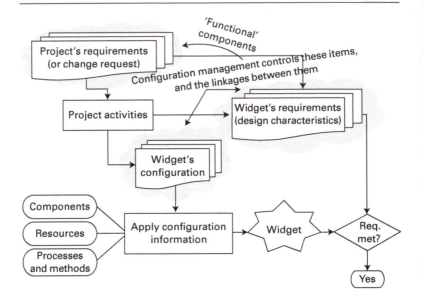

# Design traceability matrix

To make explicit the connection between features and supporting components and corresponding requirements, one creates a design traceability matrix. Recall that the RTM (requirements traceability matrix – see Chapter 6) shows us that all requirements are supported by activities and validating controls. Likewise, as we discussed staffing, we also used the RTM to make certain the people assigned to the activities are qualified for the work they are doing, given the context of the project requirements. As we can see from what we now know of configuration management, our widget itself has a similar need for traceability to the project requirements.

Here we focus on the widget's requirements and key characteristics. The design traceability matrix (or product's traceability matrix) links configuration components to the widget's features, and those features to the requirements and key characteristics that they satisfy.

The goal of the design traceability matrix is to show a link between the design of your widget and how that design meets the requirements for your widget. If you can do that, then in theory, when you make changes to the widget's design, the design traceability matrix will guide you to how changes might influence key characteristics of your widget. The reverse will also be true: if you change key characteristics of your widget, the product's traceability matrix will guide you to the affected parts of the design. The traceability matrix helps you make the needed connections in the configuration spider's web that defines your product, so you can manage the issues caused by a fly (a change) to any part of that web.

## What are key characteristics of a design?

In manufacturing, when talking about a part, the classic key design characteristics revolve around form, fit and function. The 'form' requirements specify the external characteristics of the part; its dimensions, weight, appearance, and so on. The 'fit' requirements specify how the part must interact with other parts of an assembly – how it will fit into something else; this might include tolerances and other related characteristics. The 'function' requirements specify the way in which the part must function – for example, how much load it might have to withstand, what types of stresses the part must service, exposure to environmental factors, and so on. From a classic industrial perspective (imagine we are only talking about nuts, bolts, cogs, sprockets, and those types of parts), one can effectively argue that F3 (form, fit and function) fully characterize the part.

This F3 philosophy allows one to make engineering changes to a part, or its manufacture, with minimal documentation or review. That is because this philosophy asserts that so long as the change does not alter any of the F3 characteristics, then no key characteristics of the part were changed. It is a change that functionally makes no external differences.

---

## Do-it-yourselfers already know the F3 philosophy without knowing they know it!

If you do your own car repairs, you know that many third-party suppliers also make replacement parts for your car. Typically, the third-party part costs less than the version made by the car's manufacturer. But will this third-party part be okay?

At this point, even if you had never before heard of the F3 philosophy, I bet you will find yourself considering the form, fit, function specifications of the third-party supplier's part against the specifications for the original manufacturer's version of that part, versus the impact each has on your wallet. By the F3 philosophy, if the third-party supplier's part complies with the original manufacturer's specifications, then the third-party supplier's part *should* work just fine.

Every do-it-yourselfer has to make this decision for themselves. But the point is, you might already be using the F3 philosophy without knowing that is what you are doing.

---

While the F3 philosophy may work well for many classic industrial situations, your project may be designing a post-industrial widget, or a knowledge product or knowledge widget (the widget could even have embedded smarts). So we expand what we consider as potential key features to include:

- the fashion (or process) by which the widget is created, and we may have to consider the process (or algorithm) the widget uses to fulfil its function; and

- the foundational resources used by the widget or the raw materials used to create the widget.

As mentioned above, in the pharmaceutical industry, the fashion by which pharmaceuticals are created can be a key feature of the product. Likewise, generic raw materials might not yield the same results as specified raw materials, even if the generic version is supposedly the same as the specified version:

- Many bakers understand the importance of specifying raw materials. For example, when making crème brûlée, some chefs assert that cane sugar makes for a better glazing, while sugar that comes from beets will be more problematic – even though both sugars technically meet the same chemical specifications for being sugar (Morgan, 1999). It turns out that sugar produced from beets may contain trace compounds that in this case makes a difference, and may give the glazing a faintly bitter bite (Adams, 2009).

- A classic problem with operating system upgrades is that some favourite piece of old software will not function in the new environment because some foundational component on which your favourite software relied is no longer present in the new operating system.

- The process used for choosing where the family will spend the holidays this year may be an important feature of the holiday itself. It may be my turn to spend the holidays with my parents, but if I make that assumption without first discussing it with you, and without hearing your potential alternative ideas – you might stew throughout the whole trip. We cannot hold back the tide that is the cosmic forces created by both our in-laws. The solution is virtually predefined. But how we come to that agreement is an important process, and a key feature to us getting through the holidays together.

So, depending on the project, I consider possible key features as being:

- form;
- fit;
- function;
- fashion (process); and
- foundation (things on which the widget depends to function properly).

Perhaps your industry does not need all F5 characteristics. For cogs and sprockets, F3 may be sufficient. You will need to determine the key features that apply to your industry and widget. Then, define your functional specifications for your widget in those terms. As your project designs the widget, you will want your traceability matrix to show the link between these things and how the design generated by your project addresses these things.

Admittedly, much of this is the responsibility of the designers and engineers to manage. For project managers, it is important to track the key features, or at least make certain the designers and engineers are tracking key features. If any key features change, or if a change is made in something that can be traced to a key feature, the change may have effectively created a new design/new widget (ie, this is not an incremental change). In such cases, the project manager needs to make certain that the design team does appropriate design reviews before approving a change request.

## Existing systems, implied requirements and the baseline design

A good deal of project work involves making changes to something that already exists. Widget-V01 exists, and your project is creating Widget-V02. The new version will have some *new and improved* features, characteristics, functions, or be made in a way that is somehow better.

The classic problem with this type of project is that Widget-V01 may have 'acquired' implied key characteristics. That is to say, the current design characteristics documents (assuming they exist) may not sufficiently characterize how Widget-V01 is currently being used. Widget-V01 may now be used in a way that was not originally considered when the initial design characteristics were created.

Who hasn't seen their favourite software product 'upgraded' only to discover the new version drops a feature you really liked in the older version? Was that really a 'feature' of the old version, or just a way you used it? Odds are that the 're-designers' did not realize that was even a feature, or they did not appreciate that people were using that feature.

Consider some examples of hidden or unintentional features on which people rely:

- Standard car transmissions. Hidden/unintentional feature: You can push start the car when the battery goes dead. You cannot do that with the upgraded automatic transmission.

- Old broadcast radios and old two-way radios. They connect with anyone in range, and typically have their own power. Hidden/unintentional feature: In disasters they continue to work, because they do not rely on other infrastructure, in contrast to how your streaming internet radio or cell phone works. In a disaster, other infrastructure may be gone, or networks may become overloaded; as a result, internet radio or mobile phones might not work. For this reason, your home emergency kit should include a functioning old-style broadcast radio receiver and maybe some walkie-talkies for the family to use. As for government/emergency responders, after some hard-learnt lessons, they developed several solutions to recover these features. Some now use equipment that can switch between networked services and a 'talk-around'/simplex/'walkie-talkie' mode so that in an emergency their communication devices work similarly to old broadcast units (Schrier, 2010). Also, some networks may contain ways of prioritizing 'official' cell traffic during a crisis so 'official' calls can get through, while keeping others from overloading the network (Linge, 2015).

(As an exercise, add to this list some old technology that had features or uses you miss in the upgraded version.)

If your project is making modifications to Widget-V01 it is generally advised that your design team first create an 'as-built' design traceability matrix. Here, they need to discover the current, as-built, design characteristics. Or put another way, if someone was re-inventing Widget-V01, as it is used today, what would be the requirements for that widget?

Once your team knows the design characteristics for the original version, as it is used today, they then need to understand the original widget's configuration; specifically, how the current ('as-built') configuration supports the requirements or characteristics of the widget. You will compare the proposed new configuration against this 'as-built' baseline.

Suppose you already have a baseline configuration and the design characteristics? It is good practice to pause for review of the documented characteristics, to see if any unintended user characteristics have become an implicit part of the widget's specifications. If so, review all these things with your governance team, and see if they should become part of the baseline.

Defining the baseline configuration can be one of the most important things you will do in configuration management. Theoretically, the baseline represents a working version of the widget. You must always be able to get back to the baseline, or be able to reproduce the baseline widget. By comparing changes against the baseline (or the last working version), you should be able to identify where there are issues that need to be understood in the new version. If you make comparisons to non-baseline versions, you run the risk of proliferating hidden flaws, or creating 'flaw creep'.

# Capturing the configuration and the supporting system for using it

When discussing CM systems, you will have noticed the term 'artefact' used to describe the things that represent the widget's configuration. For the purposes of discussing CM systems, we formally define an 'artefact' as an item by which some aspect of the configuration may be objectively demonstrated, defined, or otherwise determined. The CM system is the way the artefacts are captured, accessed, manipulated or used to fulfil the various needs of the change management system.

It is easy to find shopping lists of artefacts which people will say your CM system should capture. At a broad high level, we can certainly talk about capturing the artefacts that represent:

- the widget's requirements;

- the key features (as discussed above);

- the design documents (or anything that defines the widget's configuration as discussed above and depicted in Figure 10.5);

- along with the traceability matrix that shows how the key features are traceable to:

  - the various requirements; and

  - the design's aspects that support those requirements or key features.

At this level, agreement is easy. So, we continue with the easy stuff.

As the artefacts are modified, your CM system will need to capture those modifications. We call this **version control**.

In version control, we need to ask ourselves, 'Is it sufficient to capture just the new version or is there a need for explaining *in a meaningful way* what changed between the previous version and current version?' The answer depends on the software used for versioning control, your industry, and many other factors. If you decide there is a need for an explanation to accompany the new version, ask yourself, 'Who will be using that explanation and in what way will they be using it?' The explanation or annotations associated with the change should address that need. If, in practice, the explanations revert to broad sweeping generalizations, such annotations become effectively useless. As a project manager, if you start seeing too many *pro forma* annotations, one of two things is most likely happening: people are not doing their job (and important meaningful information is being lost), or annotations are redundant in this environment. (For the safety of the project, you'll need to find out which situation is occurring.)

Capturing artefacts, storing them, annotating them, and so on, is not sufficient. One must also be able to access the relevant version of the artefact when needed. This implicitly requires not only version control, but also indexing, searching and retrieval processes. It is not sufficient to have a 'write-only' database. You have to be able to find what you need in that database, retrieve it, and then use it. This is an important part of a CM system.

If you can retrieve the information, but it is not usable – well, then it is not usable. For example, at one time it may have been just fine for a previous generation to capture paper-based architectural drawings as a baseline representation of construction documents for a structural design. Then, as proposed changes to that design were considered, the documents would be checked-out, modified, and a review process would follow. There was a method in place for *using* such an approach to documentation.

As of this writing, the above-referenced design is now probably represented by a data file that is processed by computer software, which generates the construction documents, which represent the structural design. Modern data files can be more than just 'digital paper'. In the architectural field, lines that represent the 'door' (for example) are no longer just lines. Building information modelling and management software (BIMM) now attaches attributes to those lines. The attributes tell us things about the door. For example, these attributes might tell us about the physical functioning of the door, the door's characteristics (eg, the door's fire rating), among other things. Modern software also facilitates analysis of the design. Thus, the digital files themselves may be artefacts. Of course, as soon as you start capturing digital files, the version of the software that processes that file may be an artefact, and so on.

The point here is, as soon as we get more detailed than a high-level discussion, the particulars of your industry, even the particulars of your development environment, will become important to determining what artefacts you will collect, how you will collect them, store them, index them, control the version of them, and the like.

If your organization has a PMO, odds are they have a CM process defined for you, along with software for capturing artefacts. The software may also include databases for entering and managing the feature traceability matrix. Some organizations, especially organizations with larger projects, might even have people assigned to managing these things for the project. Make certain to incorporate this into your project planning.

If your organization does not have a PMO, they may still have some type of CM system defined for the organization; at very least for archiving and managing records. To the extent these things are available, use them.

If projects are small, well bounded, changes are limited, and the team is rigorous about trying to apply the principles we have outlined here, I have seen organizations do amazing things with manual efforts. Then again, even large organizations may have defined their CM processes to rely on the diligence of the team to catch issues. Learn how your organization manages such things, and leverage the established processes.

If your organization finds the concept of CM novel, new, or something they are keen to improve, study beyond this chapter will be required. When it comes to CM, the principles and goals are simple. Figuring out how to make them work effectively in your environment takes study, customization of existing tools (maybe the invention of tools), and organizational process support (the system is only good if people follow it).

## Summary points

- Product configuration (or the configuration of a widget) is the description of not only how the components of the widget are arranged, set up, interact or otherwise work to satisfy the requirements for the widget, but also may include the processes by which those components are brought together, and the resources used for doing so.

- The key features of a widget are classically described in terms of its:
  - form;
  - fit; and
  - function;

  but may need to include:
  - fashion (the process by which the widget comes to be, or the processes the widget uses to exhibit its characteristics); and
  - foundation (things on which the widget depends to function properly).

  The compilation of these specifications becomes the design characteristics or functional requirements for the widget.

- The conceptual things that typically fall under the control of a CM system are:
  - The design requirements, functional requirements, design characteristics and specifications.
  - Project requirements (to the extent appropriate – non-functional requirements may not need to be part of the product's CM system, unless they somehow drive the definition of key features).
  - Anything that plays a role in specifying the creation of the widget we will consider part of what defines the widget's

configuration. Typically, this will include things like design documents, construction documents, and so on.

- The widget's design traceability matrix. This connects the key features of our widget to the functional requirements or design characteristics that these features satisfy. It also links these features to the corresponding supporting parts of the widget's configuration information. This way, the impact of design changes on features may be directly determined, and vice versa.

- Here we use the term 'artefact' to mean an item by which some aspect of the configuration may be objectively demonstrated, defined, or otherwise determined.

- Never lose your baseline configuration. Theoretically, the baseline represents a working version (or the last working version) of the widget that satisfied a set of requirements. Always be able to get back to your baseline. Make comparisons against your baseline to avoid the introduction of hidden problems.

- Version control of artefacts is fundamental to the concept of configuration management.

- When making changes to the configuration of the widget, use the information found in the CM system to understand the impact of that change.

- If a change, or implication of a change, alters key features of the widget, you effectively have a new design. So that subsequent problems may be avoided, the project manager needs to make certain the appropriate design reviews take place.

- The skills of project management are best used to manage things. The skills of the project's designers are best used to design things. The CM system can be a great interface tool for allowing everyone to use their skills appropriately.

# *References*

Adams, C (2009) [accessed 17 October 2018] Does Beet Sugar Contain a WWII Poison? *The Straight Dope* [Online] http://www.straightdope.com/columns/read/2861/does-beet-sugar-contain-a-wwii-poison/

Linge, N (2015) [accessed 11 October 2018] When the Phones Went Dead: 7/7 Showed How Disasters Call for Tomorrow's Tech, *The Conversation* [Online] http://theconversation.com/when-the-phones-went-dead-7-7-showed-how-disasters-call-for-tomorrows-tech-44394

Marshal, R *et al* (1982) *Investigation of the Kansas City Hyatt Regency Walkways Collapse*, 1, 251–56, US Government Printing Office, Washington, DC

Morgan, M (1999) [accessed 17 October 2018] SUGAR, SUGAR / Cane and Beet Share the Same Chemistry but Act Differently in the Kitchen, *SFGATE* [Online] www.sfgate.com/news/article/SUGAR-SUGAR-Cane-and-beet-share-the-same-2939081.php

Schrier, B (2010) [accessed 11 October 2018] Why Don't Cops Just Use Cell Phones? [Online] http://schrier.wordpress.com/2010/09/09/why-dont-cops-just-use-cell-phones/

# 11

# Cost planning and cost management

People's attitudes towards money – and the associated activity – probably create the single biggest predictor regarding how they plan for expenses and manage the associated costs. In your personal life, if you have money to spare and the expense is minor, maybe you do little cost planning, if any; but if the expense is a significant cost and money is tight, you might plan things out in detail. When it comes to *managing* costs associated with your project, the same is likely true.

The attitude people have towards a project activity and their attitude towards the related money, I find to be the single biggest predictor of how good their cost planning and cost management will be. Yes, when good attitudes use poor data and poor systems, poor results follow. But with the right attitude, approach and philosophy, good project managers will:

1 maximize the tools around them;

2 be sensitive to when the data they are getting might be out of date or otherwise inappropriate;

3 develop their own tools and systems where gaps exists; and

4 dig into the data, and figure out ways to improve the information where improvement is needed.

By contrast, it will not matter how good the systems are if the attitude, approach and philosophy are poorly grounded. Systems do not a good project manager make. But a good project manager will use all the tools and systems at their disposal. When needed, they will make systems and tools to fill critical gaps.

---

### Cost management is an art, not a science

Many project management texts on the topic of cost management will detail things such as cost categories to consider, tips and tricks, and dashboard techniques. They might go into a study of analytical tools. All of these have *some* merit to *some* degree in *some* setting. Changes in the setting, however, can leave these tools irrelevant or lacking. Language, communication, etiquette and organizational effectiveness are context-sensitive arts. They are not scientific. Cost planning and management, although it may seem like simple mathematics, is also an art – because it involves the art of communicating, managing people and working with organizations.

Each business will have its own approach to implementing the specifics of this topic. To be relevant and effective, you will need to communicate using the tools and etiquette established in that environment. If you understand the principles presented here, you can map them to whatever your organization does and how it does it.

---

## Tendencies towards managing outcomes and money

Figure 11.1 shows the different tendencies people may have towards managing money and outcomes.

Looking through the 'window' of this matrix, we are considering the interaction of two variables: first, what type of money are

**Figure 11.1** Tendencies seen in managing outcomes and money

| | **Type of money** | |
|---|---|---|
| | **Your money** | **Other people's money (OPM)** |
| **Something of personal concern** | **Tendency**<br>Watch spending closely<br>Maximizes delivered value (drive for success is maximum)<br><br>1 | **Tendency**<br>Less careful spending<br>Still makes sure the goal is met<br><br>2 |
| **Done because someone else cares about it** | 3<br>**Tendency**<br>Watches spending closely<br>Compromise deliverable as needed to preserve spending limits | 4<br>**Tendency**<br>Not careful with spending (overages, expensive add-ons common)<br>Deliverable tends to miss the intent, poor quality, and delays common |

*Personal connection to the result/outcome/use*

we looking at? Is it your (personal) money, or is it other people's money (OPM)? Then we consider the connection you might have to the purpose for which that money is being spent: is it something of personal concern to you, or are you only spending the money because someone else cares about it?

Let's look at the resulting four types of attitudes and behaviours, using some close to home examples.

## 1. My money and my priority

You want to take the family on a great holiday. This trip will be epic; a family memory of a lifetime. The 'spend' is a strain on the family budget – but this trip is important for reasons your family knows best. If you watch how you spend your money, this is doable.

Without any coaching whatsoever, you will research the places to visit and you will take into account what the family enjoys doing. You are going to maximize the value of this experience. On selecting the ideal destination (or experience or whatever), you will develop the supporting details – and the details of the details. For example:

- Regarding the hotel: You've learnt that the hotel's advertised price is not what you need to budget/plan for the hotel stay. You will ask about local taxes, service fees, charges for using the amenities, shuttles to and from the airport or points of interest, and so on.

- Regarding travel: Drive or fly? If you drive, you will not have to worry about parking at the airport, luggage or rental cars, but you might lose a lot of time on the road – or is that part of the trip? If you travel by plane, at least in the United States the advertised price might not include some fees. Each airline has different luggage policies. You will make certain everyone in the family knows the luggage weight restrictions – plus, you will build in a margin for error by making certain your family is sufficiently under those limits so they can buy a few souvenirs. To make the apples-to-apples comparison between various airlines and driving, you will detail all the 'hidden' dependent, or component, charges and factors that are implied by each travel option.

- Even destination resorts or supposedly 'all-inclusive' cruises can have 'hidden' fees. And even for that 'all-inclusive' experience, you may want to plan for some 'extras'.

Think about a time in your life where you planned the cost for something significant – a holiday, wedding, birthday party, a course of studies maybe. What differences occurred between the planned cost and the final costs? How did that experience change your subsequent behaviour?

The point is, with a modicum of experience, you have learnt that the advertised price of things might not be the final, all-inclusive cost you will incur for that widget. Since this is your money, you watch how you spend it. To the extent possible, you develop an understanding of the costs you can nail down.

Now, not all costs can be planned. Some must be estimated. For example, how much will you spend on food? You make good guesstimates based on experiences or guidebooks. But you know this is just a guesstimate, so maybe you add in a margin. You expect variation from this guesstimated number. Thus, you are going to keep an eye on this component, so the variation does not get out of hand.

If, on this holiday, you find you are running over your meals budget, you might make adjustments to other things, or find a way to rein in the overage. We have had some good days of skiing. The family had a few fancy dinners out – in fact, we have been a bit too extravagant. Fortunately, a snowstorm will hit tonight. We'll order some pizzas, find a silly movie, and make it a family night around the fire. Maybe we will build a snow family at midnight in front of the lodge, when no one is looking. Suddenly, you are back on budget, and the holiday is still that epic lifetime memory you wanted!

Here is the point: if these things are true in your everyday life, your project will be no different. Just as you have to detail all the additional implied costs you incur when travelling by plane (luggage, parking, taxis or rental cars, and so on), you will have to assume that if you are buying something from a vendor (or sourcing a component of the project to someone else), there will be implied costs you need to understand. Just as in the rest of your life, you will need to monitor closely costs that are only estimated, and plan for the upper limit on that estimate. If you see overruns developing, you will need to have alternative plans for reining in those overruns.

The owner of the company, or the person who sees themselves as representing the owner(s), is probably going to have a 'my-money-my-concern' expectation towards the management of this project. It is their money. They care deeply about the success of all parts of their company; this includes your project. They want costs accurately planned, and where they cannot be planned, reasonable predictions made. They will want costs closely monitored. If a component of the spending overruns the budget, just like in your personal life, they will want adjustments made, so the overall project remains on budget.

This is the type of focus and philosophy we want to bring to managing our project. We wish everyone on our project felt as if they were spending their own money, and we wish everyone felt personally driven to the success of the project. When this happens, it is a wonderful thing. Since this is not always the case, the other quadrants are worth a review.

## 2. My priority, and other people's money

Now, instead of a dream family holiday, re-envision the project as your college-aged child going on a spring break, or some other adventure with their friends. It is something of personal concern to them: they have found the place, event, the whatever, that is the object of their epic holiday. They completely care about the outcome, so they will see to it that they achieve success. But imagine they will be using your charge cards. They have talked you into footing the bill for this trip. Effectively, they will be spending someone else's money – yours! This is the nature of the second pane (or quadrant) of our window.

You have asked your child for a cost plan. What type of plan is it? Did they plan the budget, from detailed knowledge, or did they guess-ti-plan the budget, by making a bunch of high-level guesstimates put together to *look* like a spending plan? Did they simply use what someone else has said? Is it a wish-ti-plan? All these possibilities happen in our personal lives. They also happen when you are trying to get cost planning information from others for their section of a project.

Once the trip is under way, the horror stories I have heard almost write themselves: maybe you have heard similar stories, or have a few of your own. The price for the plane tickets did not include those baggage fees. How could they have known the *unreasonable* counter person was going to charge them so much for being *only* 5 pounds (or 2 kilos) over the weight limit?! Regarding the surcharges and hotel taxes: 'Mum and Dad, I told you the room rate the hotel quoted me. Everyone has to pay that 15 per cent local resort tax. Did I have to include that in the budget *too*?' Some kids forget to see if there is a hotel shuttle service to and from the airport; taxi drivers running up the bill on *out-of-towners* is common fodder of tourist disaster stories. And even if the child is on an 'all costs included' package trip – one dear friend ranted to me about how their child went 'off tour', lost their passport and incurred more uncovered costs than one could imagine. My friend finished their rant with, 'If it was their money…' and that is exactly the point.

Being their parent, when they call you with that *minor cost overrun* what are you going to do? Disown them, cut them off completely, and leave them stranded? No. You are stuck. But one minor overrun, added to the next, and the next, eventually leads to a big cost overrun. If this is true in your personal life, again, your project will be no different. Huge cost overruns that happen all at once are organizationally easy to manage; the governance team can make a clear decision. The overruns that happen a little at a time, that you feel you just cannot say *no* to: those are the ones that will kill your project and reputation.

When people are spending OPM, they tend to gloss over spending details (especially additional expenses). Yes, there are good stewards of OPM. When you find them, cherish them! But generally, cost overruns seem to occur more commonly when people are spending OPM. There are always logical justifications for the overruns, but by the time you are hearing the justifications, it is too late. Now, if it is something they truly care about, they will still manage the 'thing' to a successful conclusion, for them, but at a cost for the person whose money they are spending. If all this is true in the rest of your life, it is probably going to be true on your project.

The point here is, you need to move people's perspective out of the type 2 quadrant thinking and into type 1 thinking. Everyone has their own gimmicks for this. You will need to find what works for your context. I like to give suppliers a bonus for under-budget completions (say 50 per cent of the difference – which sometimes can seem like a lot – but then I too have saved a lot, so why not?); and a penalty for cost overruns (once the budget is reached, hourly rates of consultants get reduced, and so on). The point is to find some way to move their attitudes and behaviours – their *connection* – back into type 1. Once you do that, the management of costs seems to run better.

## 3. My money, and other people's priority

Now imagine that by some happenstance, you are in charge of planning a holiday that includes those relatives or family friends whom you do not like (we all have them!). Need I say more? Of course, you are going to do a good and sincere job at planning this trip; you want to have a good time too. As for watching the budget, we'll assume most of the money is yours – they are included out of some familial obligation, or some other reason. How will this play out from the perspective of those disliked guests?

When someone is working on something that they do not have a personal interest in, they might miss a few essential details. Yes, they will watch the spending of the money (or a proxy for money, like time), because it is their money (their time). But maybe a desired feature of the deliverable might be left out. How could you have known your brother-in-law would be so interested in seeing the world's largest ball of twine? That was a silly thing you threw into the trip itinerary. But now your road trip is running behind schedule. Everyone is asleep in the back of the motorhome. You decided to take a shortcut and skip the ball of twine exhibit. But from your brother-in-law's perspective, that was a major selling point of the trip! He was willing to put up with your dumb stories just so he could see this claim to being the world's largest ball of twine.

Rarely are people intentionally dismissive. In the rest of your life, communicating up front what is important is… well… important! Had your relative told you about their obsession for that ball of twine exhibit (vs keeping it to themselves and expecting you should know), of course you would have stopped. Likewise, you will need to communicate to your vendors/team (and find out from your customers):

- What things, features, or components are of critical importance and expected. (Drop these and the deliverable is a failure.)

- What things, features, or components are preferred. (Dropping these things is not failure, but is not good either.)

- Which parts are desired or nice to have – but if significant delays/costs will be incurred, we can live without them.

- These are the 'extras'/'bonus' components. We would like to have them. They are not necessary. However, if you have extra time or margin, or it will not cost us anything (or cost us just a little more) and you want put a shine on that deliverable, then add this to the deliverable.

By communicating priorities up front and getting team involvement in understanding project priorities, often one can move people's connection out of this attitude and into a place where they connect better with the needs of the outcome. When we do that, things tend to go better. But even expressing needs might not be sufficient: everyone has their own way to move people out of the third attitude and into that desirable first attitude. You will need to develop approaches that work best for your environment.

## 4. Other people's money, other people's priority

Home repair contractors and car repair mechanics tend to suffer from a spotted reputation. There are many good contractors and mechanics, and it is a shame for the good ones that the others generate most of the stories heard at social events. In general, those working in this industry are working on other people's projects and spending OPM. For them, the tendency towards type 4 behaviour is strong.

Someone else cares about this bathroom renovation. Someone else cares about this car. From the contractor's/mechanic's perspective, it is *not their money*. Once the home renovation starts, if something happens that causes a cost overrun – the homeowner has to pay, and the contractor gets a percentage of that overage; so it is to the contractor's advantage to let this happen. We assume they are not doing anything intentional to cause these types of situations, but missing a little detail here – or making a proverbial mountain out of a molehill there – and suddenly this project cost is more than you expected. Will all the workmanship be Grade-A quality? Or is the quality workmanship reserved for the parts you can see? Once your car is on the rack and apart, what do you do if the mechanic says, 'Wow! Lucky I found this. XYZ is about to break. You could have been stranded.' It is not the mechanic's money, so of course they encourage you to pay for the additional repair. Have you ever had an expensive car repair done, only to discover it did not fix the problem? Or another problem surfaces – maybe accidentally induced by the other work being done? It is not the mechanic's car! It is not their money! The behaviour follows from the situation.

The motivations here do not create an environment conducive to good service and careful spending.

If this is true in other aspects of your life, then it will also be true on your projects. If you subcontract out some component of the project to another department, vendor or group, what are the dynamics in play for them? If that subcontractor is not feeling connected to the outcome – and they are spending *your* money, trouble may be nearby. You will need to re-frame their connection to the outcome of the project, and the associated spend. Combinations of techniques used to get people out of types 2 and 3 and into type 1 may be helpful. Poor quality, delays and cost overruns tend to plague type 4.

# Attitudes towards cost planning and cost management – a summary

If the project is 100 per cent yours, if you will be developing all the cost plans and every unit of spend has to go through you, the natural tendencies of the situation will direct you to a good result. Rarely, however, will this scenario be the case. You will most likely be asking others for their cost plans for their components of the project. Then you will compile those values into an overall budget for the project. Once the project is under way, others will be incurring costs and obligations. What they do will roll up to your project's budget. Their behaviour becomes your problem.

How people relate to the thing on which they are working and the money they are spending is the single biggest contributor to how accurate and thorough their cost plans will be – and how good they will be at managing the incurred costs. The best results (given the available tools) generally come from keeping people connected to the idea that it is their money and their priority. Likewise, they will tend to monitor their spending and keep it in check, to the best of their abilities, given the tools they have. If they feel it is someone else's money they are spending – or if it is not their priority – or worse, if it is both OPM and not their priority, may I suggest the results are obvious?

There are infinite suggestions about how to move people's connection with a project towards type 1 thinking, but there is no magic formula that fits all situations. You are going to have to discover what works best for the people and vendors with whom you are working. Moving the dynamics and commitment of your team into a type 1 relationship with the project is important to developing good cost plans and to successfully managing your project's costs.

# Current data, historical data, and estimates vs contracted prices

When creating the cost plan for your project, you will need to get cost information from many other people. You will need to ask:

- Are they using current data?
- Are they factoring in historical performance?
- Are they giving you an estimate or a contracted/solid cost?

## Current data

When developing a cost plan, make certain the component data used for that plan are current, or are appropriately framed for the date in which the spend will occur. A common problem I see with cost plans is old data. No one does it intentionally (I trust) – yet it sneaks in. Then everyone gets surprised by the cost overrun. Make sure your data are current.

### We all know someone who develops cost plans using outdated information

As an undergraduate, I struggled to make ends meet. Scholarships covered educational and living expenses but not much more. My grandmother would send me a few dollars to take my girlfriend to the movies; I didn't have the heart to tell her that what she sent would not even cover popcorn, let alone a movie. She was working from outdated data. Correcting her would serve no purpose; doing so would even make her feel bad because she could not do more. Instead, she got a nice thank-you card, with a short note on how things were going.

Working from outdated data is okay for families with good intentions, and for non-critical things. Business, on the other hand, needs to work from current data.

What do I mean by 'appropriately framed for the date in which the spend will occur'? They say only two things in life are certain: death and taxes. Yet, in my lifetime, inflation seems to be a close third. If in every previous year there has been a price increase for something, why will next year be different? If your project spans a year or more, the current data are not adequate. You have to plan for what that item is likely to cost *when your project will be incurring that cost*. Sometimes you can get vendors to lock in a price: if so, great. Absent that, you will need a future price prediction. Yes, no one can guarantee the future price of something. Still, within reason, it is possible to build into your cost plan adjustments for future likely prices increases. Make certain to do this.

## Historical data

Historical data are also important for managing the pricing information you get. We will discuss this more in Chapter 12 on managing the supply chain. For our purposes, here: if in the past the vendor's initial price for something was £10/unit, but at delivery, the all-in total came to £12/unit – then in the future, price information from that supplier needs to have an extra 20 per cent added to it when you are doing your cost planning.

## Estimated, or contracted, cost

This gets us to the classic discussion of estimates vs quotes (or as I now put it, estimates vs contracted prices). The problem with this discussion is that in some circles, the term quote has lost rigorous meaning (while in other areas a quote is still a *quote*!). Namely, if something is a quote or a contracted price it should be fixed; not subject to change. Regardless of the label, if many things are TBD (to be determined), subject to change, approximated, pending actual hours, and so on, then it is an estimate – not a quote or contracted price (for our purposes).

Now, contracted prices for something may have conditions under which that price could change. Understand those conditions, and make certain any triggers are linked to your change control process. If a vendor or supplier adjusts their costs, make certain your governance team approves that adjustment, and adjusts your budget accordingly (see Chapter 5).

If someone gives you an 'estimated' cost for something, it is by definition not accurate. You need to be cautious regarding how you rely on it. In statistics, we talk about the 'variance' around the mean value of a sample: the mean or average value of something does not, by itself, give you enough information to understand the sample. You also need the 'variance', or expected range around that mean, to understand the significance of that average value. The same is true for estimates. An estimate by itself is virtually meaningless; you need to know the likely range (upper and lower limits) around that estimate.

Subtle signs that an estimate is likely to be low, or otherwise off, include things like:

- The estimate does not realistically contemplate the opportunity for the final deliverable to cost less.

- Missing is the 'not to exceed' upper limit or worst-case situation.

- An explanation of the likely sources of variance about the estimated value is not included.

- There is no trigger for re-evaluation (ie, if we hit this point, something has gone wrong and we need to re-assess things).

Bottom line: to build your cost plan, you will need input from many people. Make sure you understand what they are giving you. Reserve the right to adjust information given to you, based on history, the possibility of future influencing factors, or anything else that might refine your perspective. In developing the cost plan, it is important to find the lowest (or most reasonable) values that reality is not likely to exceed. A padded budget that leaves funds unused is often viewed just as badly as a baseline budget that is overrun.

# The project plan, the components and your organization

There are many wonderful texts written about cost planning. We could follow their example, and attempt to detail all the possibilities of things that you need to consider in developing your cost plan. Such categories might include: organizational overhead costs, lawyer costs, personnel costs, labour costs, facility costs, direct material costs, tooling costs, manufacturing costs, finishing costs, shipping costs, delivery costs, installation costs, training costs – and I could go on and never list them all. Likewise, as soon as you consulted with your PMO or your management team or governance team, they would point out: 'That is not how we do it' or 'We don't account for *those* costs separately, we roll *those* costs into…', or they would criticize this text for missing a 'real world' cost critical to your industry.

Your organization will have its accounting tools and methods that they have designed to best serve your industry and your organization. Your PMO, management team and governance team will have customs and practices that they want you to follow. Connect with your PMO, get input from your management and governance team. Find out what they expect from you. Include:

- what costs to account for, how to group or arrange them, and what level of detail to go into;

- how to indicate and account for estimations, contracted costs and variance;

- what tools to use to produce and present your cost plan.

After that, almost everything else comes down to working through the project plan. This may include going through any designs to a level of detail where you can know what information is needed for you to develop your cost plan. Then you will need to put that information into the form that your organization desires.

## Cost planning tools

Many project planning tools will enable you to attach workers to specific activities and include the rate for their labour. You can attach specific costs to tasks or to summary tasks. Networked or cloud-based tools may let your team populate these values for you. Once you have detailed all the costs associated with the items in your project plan, many tools will produce a plan's cost. Learn how to use your tools, and make use of them, for this purpose.

If the tool you are required to use does not let you do this, or if it is too cumbersome, you will need to find another way to use your project plan to develop such information. Perhaps you will create a spreadsheet that mirrors this function. Your tool may have an export function that will create a list of all activities – and then you can detail the costs for each activity in the spreadsheet. This will give you the project costs that flow directly from the project plan.

## Bill of materials (BOM)

Once you have the plan's costs, there may be parts or component costs. If your project is designing something, your team might not initially know all the parts and components that they will need. Lacking specific knowledge, you will ask them for a predicted cost. The design teams will have guidelines that will help them develop reasonably accurate estimates for such things. But their results are estimates, and need to be treated as such. Get from them a range for that estimate (best case–worst case). Then closely monitor costs for that component, and make adjustments as appropriate.

In some industries, as the design team develops the design, modern design tools will create a BOM (pronounced 'bomb' – it stands for bill of materials). Depending on how the tools are set up, the BOM may automatically pull prices, vendors, typical lead times and other information from appropriate databases. If not, you will need to work with whoever is responsible in your organization for developing those details.

## Organizational costs

Once you have the plan's costs and the part costs, then there are the 'organizational' costs (often called overhead). Your project will incur these costs because of your organization's customs and practices. These costs may be loaded into your team's salaries (and are already paid) or your project may have to pay as it goes, or some mix thereof. Does your project pay for time used by the company lawyer? If you are manufacturing something, how does your organization address charges for those facilities? Office space? Desks? Supplies? I could go on, but you get the idea. Your organization will have its traditional costs that every project has to support, and associated accounting practices. Your project will be no different.

Capturing the plan's costs, part costs and organizational costs generally covers most things. But always check with your PMO and governance team to confirm that you have not missed anything.

# Cost management or driving through the rear-view mirror

Some people compare cost management systems to driving your car by only looking out the rear-view mirror. At one time, many corporate tools only gave an organization a summary of their expenditures on a periodic basis; and then only with some delay after the period in question had passed. In these cases, by the time you realized an overrun was in progress, it had been going on for some time. If you drive by looking out the rear-view mirror, by the time you see you are going off the road, you might already be in a ditch.

Much of that is fading as modern tools allow for near real-time cost tracking. However, even in these situations, a lag problem can exist. The project may have 'incurred' the liability of the cost today, but the vendor, supplier or whomever may not post that charge to your company for some time. Then your company may not pay that charge for some period. By the time it is paid, and posted against your cost centre, budget, or accounting methodology for your project, months may have passed.

Fortunately, many project planning tools now have features that allow one to post actual incurred costs against the project as the plan is being executed (this used to be a laborious effort). Networked or cloud-based tools will even allow the project team to update these values themselves – hours posted against the project as they are incurred, supplies, costs, and so on – meaning the updates are viewable by the project manager immediately. If the tool the project manager must use does not allow for this, project managers will often develop their own spreadsheets or other tools by which the team can keep the project manager informed of incurred hours and costs. Ideally, these tools can let you know where your project stands *today*. But, the reality is that people may not keep this information current, so often one job of the weekly project meeting might be to collect relevant status information. Only by finding some way to track costs and expenses as your project team incurs them can you actually drive and manage the costs associated with the project (without feeling as if you are driving by looking through the rear-view mirror).

If you successfully do this, then when the corporate accounting system finally shows the charges being posted against your project's 'cost centre' or budget, then your job as project manager is to balance the books; to make certain all the charges on the corporate system are valid and appropriate. Do they match something in your project? In any large company, errors in these postings are not uncommon; hopefully most are unintentional. Always balance your books.

## Summary points

- Systems do not a good project manager make, but a good project manager will use all the systems and tools at their disposal, and make the systems and tools they need.

- Effectively developing a cost plan requires collecting information from many other people.

- Effectively managing a cost plan requires the support of many other people.

- The single most important factor in getting accurate and complete information to create your cost plan, and in getting team support in managing costs, will be the perspective and attitude of the people with whom you are working.

  - If they have a type 1 perspective, their support will be about as good as it gets. Yes, things can still be missed, and overruns can happen, but the nature of these errors will generally be of the truly exceptional type.

  - If they have a type 2 perspective, expect cost overruns, inflated costs, etc.

  - If they have a type 3 perspective, expect the deliverable to be compromised in some way. Budgetary limits (or synonyms like time and resources) will drive the project.

  - If they have a type 4 perspective, expect compromised deliverables, poor quality, delays and cost overruns.

  Do whatever you can to move everyone working on the project to develop a type 1 perspective.

- In developing your cost plan:

  - Use current data, and consider what something is likely to cost when the spend for that thing will be incurred.

  - Consider historical performance, and adjust information given to you accordingly.

- If you are getting an estimate – get the likely range for that estimate, and develop an understanding of what factors will influence that range.

- If you are getting a contracted price for something, be cautious about what things in the contract might allow that price to change. Manage changes to contracted prices ruthlessly, as these are often a source of significant cost overruns.

- Learn how to use your project planning tools for developing a detailed cost plan, and for tracking costs as they are incurred. Also learn how to use your project planning tools for presenting summaries of the data you are tracking.

- Always balance the liabilities your project has incurred against the corporate accounting of what has been paid by your project's financial plan.

- Communicate your budget plan and incurred costs in a way that connects with the organizational culture. Using methods or representations your team will understand is better than a perfect method that leaves them confused.

# 12
# The project's supply chain plan

'I, Pencil' is an essay by Leonard Read, first published in 1958. If you are not familiar with it, I recommend looking it up. In it, the author deconstructs all the things that go into making a pencil. What is fascinating is that by the time the author finishes deconstructing the basic, common pencil, we see that numerous suppliers, domestic and international alike, are involved in sourcing the components of this most trivial item – a pencil. Clearly, the issues of complex supply chain management predate our present experience. Cross-border trade, domestic trade, and all the things some might imagine are modern inventions, are *not* modern inventions. They have been with us since the creation of commerce, as evidenced by the famous Silk Road, for example. In all this, we see that fabricating almost anything seems to involve what we call supply chain management issues: how do you get the stuff you need to be where you need it, when you need it, so you can make your widget?

The topic of supply chain management is *huge*. The larger definition and scope of supply chain management goes far beyond projects, covering general business operations, customer servicing, manufacturing, inventory strategies, logistics, and much more. We are not going to do any of that here. We are going to be utilitarian, and only look at the tip of that proverbial iceberg that serves our project.

By definition, projects are something that exceeds our unaided abilities. As such, they will typically involve many other people, groups and organizations to fill the needs of your project. For our purposes, we will refer to whatever fills the needs of something within our project as a 'supplier' (and keeping it generic, a supplier will create and deliver to us 'supplies', which covers anything from raw materials to services or the supplier's own widget). By the way, suppliers also have needs. We will not get from our suppliers what we need if they do not get what they need, and so on. Thus, when we consider how all these things link together, we could think of them as forming a chain; a chain of supplies needed to support project activities.

Our focus will be on what we need to think about to make certain all aspects of our project are supplied with what they need when they need it. What do we have to do to make certain that happens? Simply put, whatever your answer is to those questions is what will become your project's supply chain plan.

# A note on vertical integration

If your organization is vertically integrated, this means all suppliers are internal (part of your overall company). In a strongly run, well-managed, vertically integrated operation, the procurement of supplies can be greatly simplified. If everything is within the family (so to speak), certain formalities can be relaxed (eg, lawyers are probably not needed if one department is procuring supplies from another department, but you might need lawyers if external suppliers are involved). Likewise, we can optimize features and operations within the supply chain. We can develop high-quality business operations that do what is best for the overall business.

## Case Study
Ford

Henry Ford probably epitomized the vertical integration philosophy. Ford owned everything from coalmines, to iron ore mines, to rubber plantations, and so on. Raw materials went in one side of his business, from which they made parts that became Ford's cars. In such systems, it is 'easy' to know what will be needed, when and where, because theoretically you control the whole chain of events – as well as the sources that supply and support those activities. Because of the efficiencies and dynamics of how he ran his organization, Henry Ford achieved unprecedented quality and mass production of (for its time) a complicated device, at affordable prices that were previously unthinkable.

Vertical integration is not something everyone can pull off. In poorly run vertically integrated companies, oddities develop:

1 The overall management structure can become top heavy (for many reasons).

2 Some departments optimize their group's functions at the expense of other departments.

3 Internal management might become complacent towards their internal suppliers:

- We expect the internal supplier to know what we want, when we want it, even if we do not explicitly tell them.

- We expect the internal supplier to be there for us, because as the internal supplier that is their job.

- We may place demands on our internal suppliers that exceed anything we would request of an external supplier.

4 The internal suppliers might feel their internal customer has to accept what they provide, because that customer cannot go anywhere else:

- Being the sole source of something can lead to entitlement issues.

- As management treats internal suppliers poorly or takes them for granted, the internal suppliers can become disengaged, leading to poor quality, lack of timeliness and cost overruns.

I could go on, but I think you get the idea. If we were discussing this over a cup of tea or coffee, I would begin to draw analogies to family system dynamics: how effective families function vs dysfunctional families. But this is not a psychology textbook, and we are not here to re-design your organization. Still, you might take a moment to ponder the family systems analogy; I will contend that the same principles that help families function better will also help in managing your various supply chain issues.

# Take a balanced approach

In response to the difficulties of managing vertically integrated businesses, some businesses use external sources as suppliers for activities, tasks, operations, analyses, and the like, that were previously considered 'in-house-only' functions. On one level, this forces organizations to have good boundaries. When using an external entity, the organization must be explicit in what they need, when they need it, and so on. The cost of using that service becomes explicit. Thus, organizations tend to be more respectful of the outside supplier's time. And that forces an organization to be better self-managed (or so the theory goes). All this can work well, until someone gets the bright idea to select suppliers by cost alone, irrespective of quality relationships – I'm sure I don't need to explain the problems with this approach.

So, a balance of what is outsourced, in-sourced, made or bought must be found; and your project must be sensitive to this balance.

In reality, as a project manager, you will probably have little say in your organization's sourcing structure. Your organization has most likely already defined what widgets will be sourced in-house, what widgets will come from outside suppliers, what widgets will be made, and what widgets will be bought; so your project will need to operate within that structure. If your organization says that internal suppliers must be the source for some things, but you get that need filled from an outside supplier, your project may get frowned on – even if you were otherwise successful. Every organization will have a different structure; some things that might be sacrosanct in one organization might be treated with flexibility in another organization. Make certain your project lives within those boundaries as defined for your organization by getting help from your governance team, PMO and purchasing department.

## Good relationships are key

Acknowledging that all projects, suppliers and companies are different, some generic best practices do apply to all suppliers, be they internal, external, remote or local. These best practices can usually be traced simply to this: treat internal suppliers with the same courtesy as you would external suppliers, and vice versa. That might mean making sure internal suppliers have clear specifications (just as you do for external suppliers); understand their lead-time needs; stay informed of progress and difficulties; don't overload resources, and so on. The reverse is also true: developing good relationships with your external suppliers (as you might with colleagues within your organization) will only benefit you when difficulties develop – and every project eventually has difficulties.

# How to develop a supply chain plan

We will approach the issue of developing our supply chain plan in four stages: first, we will consider one discrete activity or task, with the understanding that what must be done for *one* activity will need to be done for *every* activity. Then we will look at working with suppliers in general. To improve the accuracy of the information that suppliers give you, you will need to consider their past performance. Finally, you need to develop the project's supply chain plan, and monitor it.

Before starting, let's consider where the project's supply chain plan resides. Some businesses develop a separate supply chain plan for their projects, which looks similar to the project schedule or project plan. Some businesses may have separate systems, tools and methods for managing such things. Others may choose to build the supply plan right into the project plan, showing the relevant dependency links as part of the project plan itself – after all, an activity cannot start before supplies are delivered to that activity. Some will create special project schedule activities for the function of generating the supplies needed by other activities. The procurement or creation of the needed supplies can become an activity on the project plan. (This is my personal preference, because then I can see everything in one place – but that is just a personal style, and it does not work well for all situations.)

The best solution for you depends on your organization, how it functions, the tools it uses, and its methods for tracking and managing this component. Your PMO and governance team will be a good source of information on how things are done in your organization. When you involve external suppliers, your purchasing department and your legal department may also have to be involved.

## *One discrete activity*

In our chapter on planning the project schedule, we defined five characteristics of an activity. Every activity: receives inputs, uses resources, is performed to a standard, follows a method, and generates outputs. Here, we are interested in the resources portion of that definition.

Resources can mean many things. Often in projects we think of 'human resources' as driving the activities of our project, and thus we have to develop a project staffing plan (as discussed earlier in Chapter 9). However, 'resources' can mean much more.

Resources can be:

- supplies, raw materials and needed parts;
- manufacturing facilities;
- special equipment;
- tools;

or anything else that your organization needs, besides people, to perform the tasks found on your project schedule.

## Tools to use

Project scheduling/planning tools often include features for managing, tracking and load-levelling the human resource component of your schedule (we looked at this in Chapters 8 and 9), but the equivalent functions for managing *non*-human resources are not as universally developed. Some industries do have tools for this purpose, which enable one to integrate supply chain issues into the project plan in a similar way to how project planning software manages human resource loading issues. I have also seen many home-grown or in-house-developed tools for this purpose, and some impressive repurposing of generic offerings (for example, using project planning software in clever ways, even though the software was not designed for that purpose). There *are* generic project planning tools that include a supply chain management component; but right now they are not commonplace. I suspect, with time, this feature in project planning tools will become more common, but essentially: you will have to use the tools, practices and customs that are available to you. If you don't have a tool available that does exactly what you want, part of being a project manager will be figuring out how make what you *do* have do what you need. Project managers tend to be creative; this is a place where that creativity will come in handy.

The point here is that for each of your activities – each discrete task – you will need to find out what other resources that activity or task needs. When will it need those resources? A good place to start will be to ask the people who will be doing the activity. Ask them, 'What else will you need, and by when will you need it, for that activity to be successful?' – but don't stop there.

## Remember the planning fallacy

People will tend to overlook things that they need to complete a task, and they will make assumptions about what will be available to them as they perform the task. This is, effectively, the planning fallacy (Kahneman and Tversky, 1977) that we discussed in Chapter 8, applied to supply chain planning. To avoid this problem, if the task is something that was previously done in your organization, get the people in charge of that task to look at what they needed last time they did it. Any previous documentation, purchase requests, and so on will be helpful.

If it is something new (or a new spin on an old task), ask them instead to think about doing all the steps of the task, without really doing the steps – to perform an imaginary yet thorough run-through. At each point, they should document the things that each step needs, and then document what is needed to get those things *in a timely way* (who has to be contacted, how long delivery will take, and all other considerations). Each industry and business will have different concerns; most likely, your PMO will have templates to guide this activity. Absent a PMO, your purchasing department might have some useful input. Finally, industry-specific publications might be helpful in developing some templates for your specific business.

After all the needed parts, supplies, resources and associated timings have been gathered, have each group formalize their requests. As seen in previous chapters, making a request formal, and having someone sign off on something, causes them to double-check their work. Additionally, after people have given you the list, consider letting it sit for a day or two, and asking the team if they have any last-minute updates before you finalize things. Get them to take a second look at it. A peer review (getting someone else familiar with the task to review the list) can be helpful, too – essentially, all the standard things you would normally consider doing to make certain something is thorough, complete and correct.

Once you have this information, you need to develop the plan for fulfilling this need. Will your organization be building what is needed, buying what is needed, creating it in-house, or working through an outside supplier? The people providing the requests might not always have an accurate idea about how much lead time will be needed to procure the supplies or widgets their task needs. As you work with the governance team, procurement, vendors and other departments, they might have a different perspective on what will be required to procure these supplies in a timely way. The person actually doing the work (the supplier of the needed widgets) probably has a better perspective on what it will take than the person needing the widget. Incorporate this perspective in your planning.

## Inputs, standards and controls

In our definition of an activity, I call out 'inputs' as a separate feature. Sometimes 'inputs' need to be treated as part of your supply chain plan. For example, maybe someone will tell you that to do activity ABC, they will need an updated analysis of the new XYZ component's performance. Is that analysis an input, or a resource that needs to be supplied? We could argue over these semantics, but really, we don't care about such academic nuances. For our purposes, that input needs to be supplied to the activity, and things need to happen for that input to become available. So, the development of that input needs to be planned for. Now, do you capture that as part of the project activity schedule or do you make that part of the project supply chain plan? The right answer will be whatever works best for your organization, environment, and the tools that you have at your disposal. Just make certain that somewhere you plan for it.

What we just said about 'inputs' could also be said about the 'standards' or 'controls' that govern the task at hand. Perhaps the task requires getting an updated copy of some governing codes. Maybe a new standard practice has been developed for that task. Are there new laws that need to be considered? Maybe the people doing that task need to first take a training course. It can be good to include in your supply chain plan something that checks and makes certain that standards and controls, and the training needed to perform a task, are current and understood. Yes, these things may be covered elsewhere as you developed your project plan, or staffing plan, and so on. But is there a step to *check* on current building codes, relevant laws, and such things? Projects can span significant time frames: if you know the item is covered somewhere else, fine! The point here is to use this moment to check and make certain. While double-checking can be annoying to some, it is never as bad as letting something fall through the cracks.

## Everything takes time

As you build the list of all the supplies that the activity needs to have, you will then need to determine what it will take to get those supplies to the people doing the activity. If that supply item is coming from an internal supplier, it may be appropriate to detail a set of activities that lead up to delivery. Or, if it is coming from another department (or an outside supplier), maybe all you know is that to get the supply by the date you need it, you must place the order *so many* business days before you will need it. That is called the lead time. Everything has a lead time associated with its creation or acquisition; in your project plan, maybe you will create a simple task that represents this lead time. Whatever method you use, the important thing is to make certain your plan accounts for lead times.

## *Working with suppliers*

If the needed supplies for an activity come from an outside supplier (or another department), you might think of creating and delivering those supplies as a project for that outside supplier (or for that other department). Likewise, you may even take a set of tasks within your project and assign them in aggregate to another department or supplier – and on completion, their outputs become inputs or supplies or resources that will be used by some subsequent task in your project. Essentially, you could think of the procuring of supplies for each activity as a mini-project.

The great part about using an outside supplier is that they will probably assign someone to manage the work they are doing for you – just as though it was a project for them. This means they will most likely want to formalize processes around the work they are doing for you. They will be looking for explicit requirements, scope information, quality constraints, delivery dates, delivery requirements, costs, pricing limitations, and all the rest. They may even want to form a governance team that includes representatives from your organization. Of course, everything they will be doing for their project will most likely be smaller than your project – because their project is a subset of your project. Just the same, all the things you are doing for your project will have their counterparts in the supplier's project. Of course, all this depends on the scope, size, nature, and so on, of what you are requesting from the supplier, but the parallels are typically present.

## Be explicit

The key point here is that outside suppliers (if they are smart) will work to make things as explicit as possible. They will document what they will be doing for you, and they will get you to sign off on it. At this point, you will need to have your team exercise restraint when it comes to requesting changes of the outside supplier: typically, each time your team changes something, that change will cause the supplier's price to go up, delivery delays to result, and so on. Keep a tight rein on changes. When an outside supplier is involved, they should only accept changes that have been approved by your project's change control process. Make this explicit to them: first, this limits potential for scope creep with the supplier. Second, as a change goes through your change control process, this will give you an opportunity to incorporate any cost increases or project delays – so that your project will not be penalized for these things.

We can see that it is important, when using outside suppliers, to get the requirements and all the pertinent details right the first time. In fact, with all suppliers, internal or external, giving them good requirements the first time is always important. It's just that with internal staff and internal suppliers, many think they can *get away with* 'casual', disorganized, sloppy, or ill-defined requirements, specifications, directions, and the like. Your organization wouldn't do this to an external supplier and expect good results. So do not let people do this to internal suppliers.

## Hands-off outsourcing vs micromanagement

When using an outside supplier, it is still important to have monitoring points along the way. There will often be a need for clarifications (which must not be considered changes). If they run into trouble, you will want to know as early as possible, so accommodations can be made, if possible. Also, you will need to keep them connected to the overall success of your project. They are now part of your project; you need them to know they are a valued contributor. Ignoring or losing touch with your outside suppliers, taking for granted that everything will just show up on the planned date, leaves open many opportunities for problems to develop. Many problems can be averted simply by checking in with the outside supplier to see how things are going. Stay in touch!

Hands-off outsourcing is a disaster waiting to happen, but so too is micromanagement. Finding the right balance depends on the situations at hand, the vendors with whom you are working, and the relationships involved.

Outside vendors will hopefully force your team into these best practices. Best practices protect them as much as they help you. However, not all vendors will hold you to these standards. If a vendor or supplier leaves things loose, open-ended or ill-defined, and offers to just 'work things out' as you go – this is often a precursor to later troubles. With outside vendors, hopefully, all this is a little obvious, so we won't labour these points.

The problem is that when we source work to internal organizations, for some reason project managers tend to forget all these best practices. Requirements are often left loose. Work is ill-defined, and redefined as you go (read: unmonitored changes). What started out as relaxing a few formalities can quickly run amok.

When working with internal suppliers, apply all the same best practices that you would generally use with outside suppliers. Make the requirements for their portion of the project explicit. Limit and monitor change requests. If appropriate, get someone from that internal source to act as the mini-project manager for that work. Stay regularly informed of progress, and so on.

---

**Tip**

Good practices are always good practices, but it's okay not to be overly pedantic. Do what works for your organization, in your particular situation, using best practices whenever possible.

---

## Account for past performance

Financial planners say past performance is not a guarantee of future success. They are right, of course: no one can guarantee the future. But past behaviour of people *does* correlate highly with their future behaviour. When processing information provided to you by others, you will need to discount that information to adjust for any biases that they might have. Kahneman and Tversky refer to this as de-biasing.

People generally cannot see their own biases. They will firmly believe the information they have given you is accurate to the best of their abilities. They're right – it is accurate *to the best of their abilities*. Now you need to do better than that.

One way to improve information is to 'discount' (adjust) the information people give to you, based on their past performance. If an outside supplier told you in the past that something would take 9 weeks, and then it took them 12 weeks, that's a 33.33 per cent overrun ([12 – 9] × 100/9). So this time, when they tell you it will take them 15 weeks to fabricate a part for your project, you probably need to add 33.33 per cent to their portion of the plan; ie, allocate 20 weeks for them (15 weeks + [33.33 per cent × 15 weeks] = 15 weeks + 5 weeks = 20 weeks). But be aware: *you cannot tell them you did this.*

There is an old adage that states: work expands to fill the time allotted for it. Seemingly, some people will always have a need to be just a bit late for things, no matter how much time you give them! So when building the project's supply chain plan, provide a buffer where you still hold them accountable for the delivery date they gave you, but you have free float built into your project plan so that – should they overrun the date by their 'typical' amount – things in your project will not go critical.

The same thing is true for budgeting and cost overruns. No matter how much money you allocate to a vendor, some vendors will always find a way to be just that little bit over (maybe only 10–15 per cent over – not enough that you are not going to cancel the contract on them, but it all adds up). Hold them accountable for what they tell you – but then budget based on their past performance (and don't let them know you did this – otherwise they may spend that and more again).

What if you don't have a past track record on which to base a discount factor? This situation gets dicey. You could check references – but rarely does anyone give you a bad reference. You might look at how they managed the process of getting you a quote or an estimate. You could even give them a pilot project (something small) and see how they perform on this. Of course, they will be on their best behaviour during the quote process, or if they know the small project is a test. Nevertheless, if problems are seen here, that is a good indicator you will need to discount the information that they give you.

What about internal organizations? All the same rules apply, but this can become socially sensitive, as your governance team will see what you are doing. For outside suppliers, you can easily justify buffers, especially if you have the historical information to support you. It is likely others on the governance team may have experience with that supplier. All might be supportive of you building a margin around that supplier's work. For internal suppliers, a different dynamic can develop.

Members on your governance team may also be managers for the organization whose data you are adjusting. They may feel a personal stake in that data. You tweaking the data could be seen as a direct assault on them. Be sensitive to this. It is important that they know you are not disrespecting them, but rather trying to facilitate their success. Still, if at this moment you point out, 'Every other time your department has been a few weeks late, so I thought I'd try to give you some breathing room', it is not going to go well. You're forcing them to revisit and justify all their past wrongs, and no one likes that!

Organizations are people-based entities. All the emotional, psychological, political and interpersonal dynamics that are part of people are also part of organizations. If your governance team tells you to take the slack out of the project plan, out of the supply chain plan, because *this time* we will be holding them accountable to be on time, you might not have much of a choice. Perhaps the best you can do is make certain the override is memorialized some place so that should/when trouble occurs, you can be forgiven for the kerfuffle; that you do not get the blame. This is definitely easier said than done. And maybe you can hide slack/float/free float elsewhere. Your job is to successfully complete the project – not get mired in office politics.

Keep in mind that no one is perfect. Part of the role of a project manager is to organize imperfect people, processes, systems, materials, information, and all project aspects, to create something beyond our individual abilities. One way to do this is to build in allowances for imperfections. Sometimes, in the absence of data, figuring out what that allowance needs to be ends up relying on a 'gut feeling', experience, craft or wisdom. Use data when possible, get input from your team, and use your skills and experiences – but always try to develop a 'fault tolerant' supply chain plan.

## Build and monitor your supply chain plan

After you have collected the relevant information for every activity, you will need to build your supply chain plan (in reality, you are probably building the plan as you collect the information). How you build your project's supply chain plan, and what systems you use, depend on the environment in which you are working. Of course, you will have to use whatever tools the organization requires.

While sometimes this can create double work, I tend to prefer at least highlighting the key steps of the various supply chain components on the project schedule itself. Specifically:

- when do supplies need to be ordered;
- when does work on a supply need to start;
- what lead times are important;
- when is a supplier planning to complete work on their portions;
- where is there free float in the plan;

and so on.

This way, I can see everything in one spot. The problem with this approach is that if something needs to be changed, I may have to make the changes in two places: on the project schedule, and in whatever organizational tools I am also using. This becomes a *real* problem if the other tools are dynamic: if people or systems other than me can change things in those other tools. For example, the factory may have its own scheduling tools. Certain tasks may need time on certain machines. If the factory scheduler changes your time slots, how do you keep their changes synchronized with your 'master plan'? Keeping multiple systems/tools synchronized is always problematic, and requires manual effort, until such things are automatically integrated. Bottom line here: do what works for you and your environment.

Once you have a supply chain plan, you will need to monitor it, and the things that affect it. Build periodic checkpoints into all your processes. You don't want these checkpoints to be too frequent, because that can create additional work which in itself slows down the project. However, too few can leave you vulnerable. What's the right balance? We discuss this more in Chapter 13, under the heading 'Tracking frequency'. All the concepts mentioned there also apply to supply chain monitoring.

## Summary points

- Even the simplest of projects can have involved supply chain issues that need to be managed. Overlooking this component of your project could be a cause of project failure.

- At its most basic, a supply chain plan can be designed like so:

  - Review all the activities in your project plan.

  - For each activity to be successful, what needs to be provided to it, by when?

  - Develop a plan for achieving the above, and make sure you monitor it.

- Treat all suppliers (internal or external) with best practices. This means things like:

  - making requirements explicit;

  - allowing for adequate lead time;

  - limiting changes to only what is absolutely necessary and approved.

- Outside suppliers often treat the provisioning of their goods and services to you as a mini-project. The formal processes they bring to the table can be helpful:

  - Apply such processes to internal suppliers when possible.

- – Be suspicious of suppliers who want to keep things loose, vague, ill-defined, open-ended, etc.

- When developing your plans, review the past performance of suppliers against actual historical outcomes. De-bias currently provided information to account for differences seen between past estimates and actual past performance. Pay particular attention to lead times, duration, cost estimates, and the like.

- When creating your project's supply chain plan, it can be worth the extra work to highlight on the project schedule, or the master project plan, the key parameters and checkpoints of various procurement activities, vendor activities and supplier activities, even if your organization has other supporting tools for tracking these things. Being able to see everything in one place is valuable.

- Monitor suppliers while they are in the process of provisioning your team. If you check in too often, that can become a hindrance. Not often enough, and you can let problems fester. You will need to find the right balance so you uncover problems before they become critical.

## Reference

Kahneman, D and Tversky, A (1977) *Intuitive Prediction: Biases and corrective procedures*, Technical Report PTR-1042-77-6, Advanced Decision Technology, Defense Advanced Research Projects Agency, Office of Naval Research, United States

# 13

# Project execution

## Tracking, updating, reporting and acceptance

At this point, you have accomplished a lot:

- You have taken on an endeavour that, by definition, is beyond the unaided abilities of the average person. With tools, processes, a team, or a combination of all these things, you have corralled a task that is beyond your own abilities.

- You have identified where in the organization you and this effort fit.

- You have developed a governance team to advise and help your project be successful.

- You have defined the scope, the requirements, the deliverables and the acceptance criteria. You have created a plan for achieving what defines quality for your project. You have got buy-in and support for all these things.

- You have defined the project lifecycle that best fits the various components of your project. You're even applying different lifecycles at different points. You have created a schedule for performing the activities that need doing, so that this job can get done.

- You have created a staffing plan. The appropriately qualified people are assigned to the activities.

- You have created a plan for identifying the important parts and characteristics of whatever it is your project is designing or building or doing. These key characteristics of what your project is developing include things such as the widget's form, fit, function, fashion (or key processes involved in your design) and the foundation of your design (the things on which your project's widget depends as part of its design). You have created a plan or method for capturing these configuration issues. Likewise, you have established processes or reviews so that when changes are proposed, your team can determine if important characteristics are impacted.

- You have worked to get people to own the cost issues associated with this project. They have given you good cost data, and they are committed to helping you manage the project to keep it within the defined budget.

- You have figured out how to get all the supplies and resources needed for your project to where they will be needed, when they will be needed.

In an ideal world, you have plans to make all these things work, your plans are flawless and the team simply needs to execute them. Of course, none of us lives in an ideal world. Just because you've defined what *should* happen, doesn't mean that it *will* happen.

## The best-laid plans

The real world is filled with 'natural variation'. With few exceptions, it is virtually impossible to make anything happen exactly; everything happens with variation. When it comes to executing your project plans, you will need to define acceptable levels of tolerance for the activities, widgets and performance criteria of your project. Even after this, it is still possible for all the components of something to be 'acceptable' (ie, within an acceptable level of tolerance for that component) and yet for the overall result to be 'unacceptable'. Tolerance assumes that there will be random variation about the desired value, meaning some components will be on the negative side of the desired value, and some components will be on the positive side of the desired value. But suppose the error is always in one direction?

Imagine you are running a doctor's surgery (physician's office). You schedule appointments to be 30 minutes long ±15 minutes. You expect some patients will be processed quickly, only requiring 15 minutes of the doctor's time; but others might require 45 minutes. If the doctor's contact with the previous patient runs 15 minutes long, no one will mind a 15-minute delay for their appointment, so this scheme seems acceptable. However, if the doctor runs 15 minutes long on *every* patient, then within four patients the doctor will be running an hour behind schedule. Each previous patient was managed within the acceptable level of variance, but the *overall* implementation of how the surgery (office) is being run is now unacceptably behind schedule. The tolerance errors add up to become intolerable.

When acceptable variation always seems to happen in one direction, this is called bias. In project implementation, bias errors are serious, because no one thing is unacceptable – there is no one thing to correct – and technically nothing needs correction, because everything is acceptable. But as the biases add up, the overall project can end up like the above doctor's surgery (physician's office) – egregiously behind schedule (or over budget, poor quality…). If you see bias problems developing, this could be motivation for a general re-assessment and re-planning of your project; or a re-framing moment with the task performers. Consult your governance team if you see this problem developing.

# Monitoring and re-planning

Natural variation and creeping bias errors are not our only problems. The unexpected happens to every project. Despite everyone's best efforts, something will go wrong: a storm closes a plant, a strike occurs, equipment malfunctions, the lead designer quits or falls ill, *stuff happens*. It is the project manager's job to figure out how to keep the project on track. Thus, one must know how the project is performing in comparison to the plan, budget and quality objectives/acceptance criteria, so developing issues get addressed before they become problems. As discussed throughout, the tools you are using will be important to helping you in these pursuits. Be familiar with your tools. Use your tools to facilitate your monitoring and tracking of the project's many aspects.

As you see deviations developing, you may decide re-planning is essential. The first rule of re-planning is never to lose your baseline. Also, always understand the root cause for the re-planning need. These three things (the baseline, the causes for re-planning, and what finally actually happened) become the focus of Chapter 14, where we will discuss the evaluation of your project. During project execution, however, these things help keep projects focused on their defined purposes and limit the potential for scope creep. Always go back to the baseline for all comparisons. That will let you know how far things have gone astray, and if it is time to rein in these changes.

Next, it is important to keep the governance team informed of progress, problems and planning modifications. While all changes should be going through the change control process, you will also need to keep the governance team generally informed about the project's status (more on this below when we discuss upward reporting).

Lastly, when you developed the requirements, you also defined deliverables and acceptance criteria. As your project enters its final stages, it becomes essential that your project delivers the deliverables and satisfies the acceptance criteria. Near the end of any project, there always seems to be a debate if one more thing is needed, if something else should be included, or is the job really finished? If your project has delivered the deliverables and met the acceptance criteria, then there should be no debate: the work is done. The project's efforts should be found acceptable. If the acceptance criteria are demonstrated by an objective measure, then sign-off becomes a formality. More on this when we discuss getting acceptance.

# Tracking frequency

Putting the cultural issues aside, I start thinking about this problem from the perspective of something called the Nyquist rate. Harry Nyquist is the electrical engineer who, after a lot of nifty maths, discovered that to digitize an analogue signal, you need to sample it at (at least) twice the speed of the fastest-changing component found in the original analogue signal. This is why, when they invented CDs (or other forms of digital recording), for a non-lossy reproduction they sample the signal at something greater than 40 KHz – twice the 20 KHz which marks the highest frequency humans can hear. For us, the relevant question is: how fast will things be changing on the tasks of your project?

Applying this concept to projects, you will want to sample tasks more frequently when significant changes are happening, and simply monitor/check in (less frequently) during times of slow change. If nothing significant is expected to be happening, asking for detailed progress reports can be annoying. At the same time, a simple 'check-in' to make certain that problems have not developed can be appropriate. As project managers, we craft the type of sampling needed to fit the situation.

Note: Through the rest of this section, the term activity is used synonymously with 'summary activity'. Checking on each activity atom (as described below) could be overdoing it. Looking at the summary activity as a whole, and the significant points within that summary activity, is often more useful and practical. You will need to determine the right balance based on the structure of your project plan.

As each activity (summary activity) starts, you will want to check in with the people assigned to that activity, to make certain it starts okay. As each activity closes, you will want to make certain the activity has been successfully finished. During the performance of the activity, are there significant milestones where progress reports would be insightful? Obviously, getting updates at those points is important. Then, applying the concept of

Nyquist sampling, a check-in between these points can be appropriate.

Asking for too many reports creates excessive overhead and hurts the project. Too few lets things get out of control. For example:

- If an activity starts on 1 February and ends on 28 February, and there is a significant milestone at the halfway point on 14 February, then we check in at these three points. Did everything start okay? Is that milestone status looking good? Did everything complete successfully?

- Now, with a hat-tip to Nyquist, we do a quick check-in halfway between all these points, say, on the 7th and the 21st. At these additional points, you just want to make certain no problems are developing.

# Types of check-in

As alluded to above, not all check-ins are created equal. Each check-in has a different purpose; some might need a full team meeting or report, while others might only require a quick chat with the team lead. And everything in between is possible. Craft the check-in to fit the need.

Your goal is to sample the team's perspective of how the activity is going. You're not trying to micromanage or get in the team's way. You're trying to get a sense of the project's state, and detect if any problems, needs or other support issues are developing, before a serious problem occurs. *The easiest problem to fix is the one you avoid.*

## Humanistic approach

Remember these are people doing the work. They are there to get the task done, not to create reports for the project manager. If applying 'Nyquist'-like logic has you checking in every day, and nothing significant is changing, you are probably overdoing it. Yes, in certain Agile environments daily check-ins are part of some methods, but that is unique to that approach. Rather, in such a situation, pause. Consult with the team lead for the activity. Sort out an appropriate check-in schedule that lets them get work done, while keeping you informed. Let's call this a humanistic approach, because it is based on human contact and acknowledging that humans are doing the work.

## Analytical approach

Another method project managers use to track tasks I will call the analytical approach. Here, you track the time *worked* against the task and compare it to the total amount of time *allotted* for the task. Then you compare them both to the percentage of the task that is completed.

Much of this type of tracking can be automated using network- or cloud-based tools; they integrate time reporting and the team's inputs into the master project schedule. Even if your project planning/scheduling tool is not network/cloud based, it will typically have the ability for you to enter this type of data manually.

From the hours worked against a task, compared to the hours scheduled for that task, and along with information about what percentage of the task is completed, your planning tool can generate analytical indicators. Broadly, if a project manager sees that 75 per cent of the person-hours scheduled for a task have been booked against that task, but only 25 per cent of the task has been completed, that can be a flag that something is going wrong with that task.

Theoretically, the analytical approach has great merit. However, the social dynamics of this approach can create a mirage of success – because it relies on data to represent the absolute state of a human-based thing; people-based things are rarely absolute. This method often yields false positive status reports. It may show 75 per cent of time booked against an activity, with 75 per cent of the activity completed; all is good! What is missing is that the last

25 per cent of the activity may be the hardest part – despite the on-track analytics, the activity may actually be in trouble!

---

### Beware of manufactured heroes

The key component of what I call a 'manufactured hero' is that *they themselves* contributed to the crisis that they heroically solve. If someone is rewarded for fixing a crisis, *more* than for doing the work to avoid a crisis, then organizations can quickly devolve into hero-driven behaviours vs a team of reliable doers. The temptation to gain praise and approbation for a heroic resolution of a crisis (which they let happen in the first place) is even greater if they're not likely to get recognition for the good job that prevents crises! It may sound counterintuitive, but 'heroes' (especially of this type) can be a project manager's worst nightmare – especially in immature organizations that do not recognize this as a problem.

---

Each approach to tracking and monitoring project activities (humanistic monitoring and analytical monitoring) has its short-comings and merits. The two used together seem to complement each other well. Stay connected to the people doing the activities, so you can get a sense of how the activity is going. Analytics can quantify what you learn from your contact with the team. They can also help you deduce things that might not be obvious from your contacts with the team. And, relationships you develop through your contact with the team will help you deduce if the analytical data you are getting makes sense.

## Keeping everyone up to date

As you get information from activity performers and track what is going on, you also need to keep the team informed of what is happening in general. If things have to be rescheduled, people work better with adequate warning and with a perspective on why things are being rescheduled.

A word about 'adequate advance warning': it can be helpful to think of tasks as having a 'halo' around them. There is the time leading up to a task, and then there is the time following a task. People do not just start doing anything instantly. We tend to think about what will be happening and get ourselves in a mental framework for that event. Then, after an event, we do not instantly turn off. Some 'ramp-down' re-adjustment time follows, as we move on to the next thing. Some project managers include this 'halo' on the project schedule. For tasks involving specific preparations, or set-ups, this is important. Others do not show this halo separately; it is just implied by the organizational norms. Either way, if you reschedule a task during the intro-halo period (or worse, after the task has started), this can be disconcerting and counterproductive. Avoid doing that whenever possible.

Also, avoid schedule churn. Once people see the project schedule, they will start planning other aspects of their lives around it: holidays, work for other efforts, and more. Without knowing it, your schedule change can cause negative repercussions about which you are unaware. Despite all good intentions on your part, these negative repercussions can come back to haunt you (low morale, disgruntled feelings, lack of respect for your skill…). When a change in schedule is needed, work to get buy-in from the people impacted by the change. It is important to keep the team informed so they can accommodate changes as the need develops.

Schedule changes do not happen independently. Any change in schedule may impact your staffing plan, your resource plan, your supply chain plan, or it may have budgetary impacts. When changing your project schedule, remember to adjust all related aspects of your project.

# Upward reporting: frequency, purpose, structure and style

While every organization is different, there are some generalities that apply to many upward-reporting situations. This includes things like reporting to the governance team and other departments.

## Frequency

Upward reporting is a reverse Nyquist problem. Here you need to construct meaningful information (the signal, if you will) from all the data that you are gathering. Then report that meaningful summary, indications or needs that are derived from the information you have gathered. As a result, upward meetings are less frequent, but require that you report substantive information.

Schedule your reports to the governance team so that when you meet, your reporting will be communicating meaningful information, be asking for substantive help, needed coordination, or something worthy of such a gathering. It never hurts to ask the governance team how often they would like to meet; if you are doing what they want you to do, it is much harder to be doing something wrong.

## Purpose

Typical governance team concerns include:

- Are we on schedule?
- How are expenses tracking against the plan?
- Are there potential issues that need to be addressed?

Make certain to address these points in your upward reports, and include anything else that the governance team may request. Ask them if they would like to add anything to your standard report. If your organization has a PMO, they may have templates to guide such reporting.

As a project manager, remember that the governance team, management teams and the higher-ups are there to help your project with governance, management or organizational issues that are beyond the scope of your purview as project manager. Make use of this resource when needed – and be clear about what your project needs to be successful. These will form the list of things that, from your perspective, you will want to make certain are included in any upward reports.

## Structure

There are many texts on how to run good meetings. Find one you like. Study it. Develop your skill at running good meetings. In the meantime, for governance team meetings, at least cover the following basics:

- Know the purpose of the meeting. Have defined goals for the meeting. If the meeting does not have a clearly defined goal, strongly consider not having the meeting.

- Publish an agenda in advance. Include the goals/purpose for the meeting. Think of a meeting as a micro-project. The meeting goals are equivalent to the scope/requirements document. The agenda is analogous to the project schedule plan by which you hope to satisfy the goals/purpose for the meeting. If the stated goals/purpose is met, the meeting is a success. In the advance information you send to the attendees, include enough detail so people can come prepared. Make certain the right people will be attending.

- Maintain structure and control during the meeting. Considering the attendees, the time cost of this meeting may be significant.

- Record decisions, action items, responsible people, etc. Then immediately publish this to all attendees, asking for corrections. If there are any misunderstandings about these things, you need to resolve those misunderstandings right away. This published perspective guides not only your next activities, but also others on whom your project depends.

## Style of your presentations

Style your presentation for effective business communication. This means starting with the point of your analysis, and including what you are going to be asking for, or need, right up front. Hopefully, prior to the meeting, you have already sent your presentation to attendees, and they have reviewed it. If everyone already agrees, and there is no need for discussion, then your meeting may be over in minutes. Rarely do people get upset about a meeting ending early!

Once you have made your point, get into the logic that got you to that point. If needed, get into the data that support that logic. At any time in this process, as soon as the attendees agree with your logic (or if the team wants you to try finding a different approach), it is not uncommon for the governance team to cut the project manager's presentation short. Suddenly you might hear 'Got it!' followed by 'Here's what we will do…' or 'Here's what we want you to do…'. Then everyone moves on to the next issue. Don't let this unnerve you: this is not about you putting on a show; it's about getting business done.

### The Pyramid Principle

The presentation structure described in this chapter is an oversimplification of a method called the Pyramid Principle. You can find out more about it in Barbara Minto's *The Minto Pyramid Principle: Logic in writing, thinking and problem solving* (1996). Briefly, the Pyramid Principle inverts the typical storytelling process. Most people tell stories by starting with the details. They develop arguments, building to the punchline. This is great for telling tales around the campfire, but in business this approach is expensive, wasteful and can lead to much confusion. At the beginning of your tale, no one knows where you are going, so they do not know what to think of the information you are telling them. Everyone may interpret your information in different, irrelevant ways.

In Minto's method, you start with the main point (the point of the pyramid). Now people know how to frame what you are presenting. Each level of development in your presentation is more expansive than the previous – like a pyramid. At any point, if agreement is reached, there is no need to spend more time on this topic; we can move on to the next topic.

For reports to governance team, business communications, and developing winning business presentations, the Pyramid Principle style connects effectively with many business executives. Many project managers will find Minto's text helpful in developing their upward presentations and communications.

# Getting acceptance

The conclusion of every project can be one of the toughest moments a project will face. At the end of a project, one must get acceptance of the work that has been done, so that the project may be closed.

If the project has been run badly, the end of the project will be filled with disputes about what is still open, undone work, poor quality, late deliverables, and so on. There is nothing worse than being a project manager over a failed project. A whole niche cottage industry has developed around cleaning-up and closing-out badly run projects, giving rise to so-called 'fix-it' project managers and consultants.

If your project has been run well and is successful, an odd thing happens: people will want to keep it running. There will be last-minute requests for *just one more thing*. If you are under budget, there will be compelling arguments to do more with the remaining money. If the project is wrapping up ahead of schedule, people will want to use that time to explore options and additions. Such successes can be very heady. There will be seductive 'Siren Songs' encouraging you to polish this apple just a bit more. Unfortunately, despite all the best of intentions, such efforts usually end up bruising the apple.

The way people work to snatch failure from the jaws of victory can be dumbfounding; yet, if you take time to analyse it, the dynamics and results make sense. What accounted for the success of the project was the long planning, enduring effort, the thoughtful and thorough execution by all (and many more things). At the end of a well-run project, it appears that such success *just happened*, and it can be overwhelmingly tempting to try to capitalize on that success with a few extras. These last-minute whims have none of the properties that led to the success of the overall project. If you try to implement them, it will be anyone's guess if they will really help your project, or will they be what undoes all your good work and creates a project failure?

My personal view is one must resist the temptation of project-closing Siren Songs to do just one more thing. Like Homer tied to the mast of his ship, you will need to stay tied to the original requirements and the formal change control process. The extras that people will try to sneak in at the last minute of an otherwise successful project are dangerous. If these things are truly desired, they will be best used as seeds for the next project. Let this project end!

So now, how do you get acceptance for the work the project has done? How do you close out your project?

Back in Chapter 5, we discussed defining the project scope. A critical part of the project's scope was defining acceptance criteria. We also made the point that acceptance criteria, whenever possible, need to be precise and clear. We noted that the more you make your acceptance criteria specific, measurable and objective, the better off you will be. Well – this is the moment that 'better off' happens! Here, everything will come down to one question: have you met all the acceptance criteria?

If the answer to this question is open to interpretation, you are in trouble. You already believe that all the efforts of the project satisfy the acceptance criteria, otherwise you would not now be at this point. The 'client', customer or whoever will be 'accepting' this project will see things through their own eyes (as we all do). They may interpret the acceptance criteria in a way that favours their position – which may have you and your team doing more work (possibly for no more pay); or worse, your organization might not even be fully paid for the work that was done.

A well-defined, precise, clear, measurable, objective scope document is your best friend. If you did this correctly at the beginning of the project, and kept the team's efforts focused on work that led to satisfying the acceptance criteria, then you already know if your project will be successfully accepted. All you need to do is present the tests and data showing that – *objectively speaking* – your project has satisfied the acceptance criteria, and sign-offs should become a formality.

Each organization will have its own rituals, formalities and customs for managing this moment. Work with your governance team to arrange for such appropriate close-out, completion or acceptance meetings, events, handoffs to the customer, and all that. Close out the project in whatever way is appropriate for your environment.

## Summary points

- No plans are perfect; people will deviate from plans, reality will not occur exactly as planned, and troubles befall every project.

- Track tasks and activities frequently enough so you can accurately represent what is happening in your project, but avoid checking in with people so frequently that you become a problem. Finding the right balance takes some understanding of how fast things will be changing on a task, and some organizational sensitivity to how your environment works.

- The goal of monitoring is to find developing issues before they become problems. The easiest problem to fix is the one you avoid!

- Use both a humanistic approach and an analytical approach to stay connected to what is going on in your project, and to summarize the status of your project.

- Who gets the best rewards in your organization? Manufactured heroes? Or doers? Your project will get more of whatever you reward.

- Keep everyone informed.

- When changes are needed, get buy-in from the people impacted by the changes. Avoid churn whenever possible.

- Be efficient and effective with your upward reporting. See *The Pyramid Principle* as one way to improve such business communications and presentations.

- Well-defined, precise, clear, measurable, objective scope and requirement documents are your best friend as a project nears closure.

- Get acceptance sign-offs, close out your project, let it end. Any desires for more features, additions, and just one more thing can become good material for a follow-on project. But for this project, stick to the requirements and scope as defined, and bring it to a successful end!

## Reference

Minto, B (1996) *The Minto Pyramid Principle: Logic in writing, thinking and problem solving*, Minto International Inc, London

# 14

# Evaluation, lessons learnt and improving the next project

*All improvement happens project by project and in no other way.*

Joseph M Juran

Picture this. It is early morning. You're half-awake, shuffling down a jetway towards your plane. People are casually chatting on their phones, to each other, reading, or just vacantly staring at the line in front of them. As you near the plane, out the jetway window, you see a buzz of focused activities. Luggage is being loaded; fuelling is under way; someone is checking something on the plane; the food services truck is delivering snacks you'll be grateful for an hour from now. At the door to the plane, the attendant interrupts your gaze. With a practised smile, they greet you and ask where you're seated. As you look up, you see that behind the welcoming attendant is their partner busily locking a coffee pot into place, securing the carts and galley doors. You peek into the cockpit; the number of gauges and switches is overwhelming. One pilot is reciting a checklist, while the other pilot seems to be repeating everything. You hear the test of an alarm. As you work your way back to your seat, a maintenance person headed to the cockpit squeezes by you with a clipboard in hand, containing a form for the pilot to sign. You find your seat and settle in. The doors are closed, and the attendants are telling you how to fasten your seatbelt. You wonder, *who does not know how to fasten a seatbelt?* Then the attendants walk up and down the aisle, checking seatbelts, telling people to put their trays up and clear the space at their feet. Next thing you know, you are airborne and above the clouds, at 35,000 feet. Soon after a boring flight that seems to have taken too long, you arrive safely. As you exit the concourse, your party spots you. You're glad to see each other. As you get in the car, they ask, 'By the way, how was your flight?' You shrug. It's no big deal: 'Eh. It's a flight. It was uneventful.'

What you just shrugged off is virtually impossible in any other aspect of your life. Yet in the United States alone, it happens tens of thousands of times a day, with typically the same, uneventful, boring results. The number of things that had to come together to make that flight happen is dumbfounding. As we have seen, even trying to coordinate just a few things to make a small project happen can be challenging, complex, and fraught with difficulties.

Consider just the obvious things we saw in the above flight. It is important to properly load the luggage so the centre of gravity of the plane is balanced – otherwise the plane won't fly too well. How the cargo doors are closed is critical; if they accidentally open in flight, it will be a really bad day. There is a specific process for fuelling the plane, so that naturally occurring static electricity does not start a fire and blow the thing up while you are still on the ground. Galley items have to be secured so that while the plane is taking off, or if in-flight turbulence hits, they don't fly around and injure someone. How the maintenance crew accomplishes their job is guided by forms and processes to make certain no bolt is left untightened (figuratively speaking). Those seatbelt demos and all the checks the flight attendants do (which you might sometimes find annoying) are crucially important – should something go wrong. In the event of a problem, all these processes are critical to saving your life. And finally, that boring banter of the pilots following a scripted checklist, with their partner making certain they checked the things on the checklist, is actually what makes operating this complex machine even conceivable.

# Evaluate like an airline

While many things account for modern airline safety, there are four concepts that we can directly apply to improving our next project: checklists; teaming; a focus on improving systems and processes (vs punishing people); and finding and fixing issues before they become problems.

Around 1935, the complexity of flying a 'modern' plane exceeded the ability to train people. The unaided ability of humans when faced with such complexity could never be 100 per cent; complexity could overwhelm the unaided person, despite the best training. There were just too many things to consider, recall, and balance in order to fly these new planes safely. (Does this sound familiar? Remember our definition of a project – that it goes beyond the unaided abilities of one person.)

In response to this problem, the pilot's checklist was born. The checklist distils lessons learnt, experiences, problem resolution methods, and much more, into definitive actions that guide the pilot. The checklist advanced aviation into a new era of equipment.

Eventually, even an individual armed with a checklist can be overwhelmed, and major airlines developed a team approach to safety. Not only do two sets of eyes confirm anything that is important, but the flight crew as a whole work together. No one person can make a flight safe; it takes a team.

When a problem occurs (crash, mishap or kerfuffle), aviation reviews mostly go beyond chastising individuals. The revolutionary aspect of the aviation review is to own that *how* the problem developed is in itself a problem. Sometimes more training can help, and education programmes are changed; but we have already acknowledged that there are limits to this. Aviation reviews look at how better processes or equipment modifications might prevent such a problem from happening again, even if someone makes a mistake. You will never eliminate the inherent shortcomings of a single person, but typically, there is a chain of events that happen between the occurrence of a mistake and the development of a problem. Break that chain, and mistakes do not become problems.

Lastly, major airlines go one step further: they encourage identification of things that could become problems, even if no crash, mishap or kerfuffle occurred. Crucially, people are not punished for identifying mistakes, goofs, errors and problems – even if they are the ones that did it, and that is how they discovered it. The most important thing is to avoid future problems throughout the entire fleet.

In my opinion, these four things – checklists, teaming, a systems/process focus (vs a people punishment approach), and finding and fixing issues before they become problems – are nothing short of revolutionary. They enable a person to become more than themselves, to access the intelligence of all that has gone before them, and the intelligence of all those around them. The classic Isaac Newton quote says: 'If I have seen further than others, it is by standing on the shoulders of giants.' Pilots – using checklists, teams, processes and lessons learnt by others – are truly standing on the shoulders of giants.

## The checklist manifesto

For a more studied perspective on the power of checklists, one of my favourite reads is *The Checklist Manifesto: How to get things right* by Atul Gawande. His focus is on medical care, but it is well written, so I think that you will see how the lessons discussed there could be applied to almost any industry, including yours – and your job as project manager. Likewise, everything said about checklists also applies to well-constructed forms, templates, flows and processes.

So, as a project manager, where can you get these checklists, flows, well-constructed forms, templates and processes? Where do they come from in the first place? Those questions beg us to bookend our discussion seen in the first couple of chapters:

- Where does a project manager's evaluation fit in an organization?
- What does it take for you to *not so accidentally* be a better and better project manager – so eventually your projects become as boringly successful as the average commercial flight?

# Where does an evaluation fit?

Project evaluations mostly occur at the end of a project, although you probably captured much of the needed information during the life of the project. Plus, there may have been components of the project where it was important to do a mini-review on a component, activity or task that just closed out, while all was fresh in the mind.

If your organization has a PMO, they have probably already defined the framework, ground rules, and timing for conducting an evaluation. They may call it something else; for example, Lessons Learnt, Postmortem, Project Review, Project Feedback. The name is irrelevant; either way, the organization takes a moment to study how things went on the project, with an eye to doing better next time.

## How much time should be allowed for a review?

This is a subset of a much larger topic on 'organization slack'. How much spare time – seemingly unproductive time – should be built into an organization for the development of creativity and learning? There are varying opinions on this, but suffice it to say that some time needs to be budgeted at the end of a project for clean-up, generating corresponding documentation, and filing results in a useful way so that they can be easily found and used later. Your request for a post-project analysis needs to fit into the organization's preconceived notions on organizational slack, because not every organization will view project evaluations as a productive use of time (despite anything I say here). If you have a PMO, they will most likely have run this gauntlet for you already. If you do not have a PMO, then establishing time for a project review will be something you need to sort out with your governance team.

For the initial contact and review time, I like to use 5 per cent of the project duration rounded up to the nearest whole week. For example, 5 per cent of a 50-week project would be 2.5 weeks. I will round this up to three weeks, and reserve three weeks at the close of such a project for post-project analysis. The findings from that initial analysis may spur other developments, but to be clear, the point of the initial review is simply to *identify findings* – not to work or solve whatever is found. Processing, resolving and closing the findings may be handled separately, based on what is discovered. Implementation of solutions that resolve identified issues can range from the quick and easy to significant efforts, depending on what is resolved; and that is why implementation is usually handled separately from the analysis.

## What are typical goals of the evaluation?

You can probably state this as well as the next person:

- What did not go so well and why?
- What worked well on the project that the organization can use in other projects?
- Identify significant differences between plan and actual results for: timing, cost, vendor expectations, groups, and the like. What led to these differences? What parties were reliable and met their targets?
- What alternative measures could be taken to mitigate problems?
- How might current forms, checklists, templates, standards, tools or procedures be modified (or created) to help in the future?
- Could organizational changes and recommendations be helpful?

Your PMO will have their own checklist and guidelines, but absent that, start by considering the above things and develop the review process as needed, based on your experience with your project.

As project manager, much of the data needed for an evaluation is probably already in your hands. However, a project is a team effort. Your perception of what happened and why might differ greatly from the perspective of others. Make a point of scheduling time to get input and suggestions from team members – especially those working on components that did not go so well.

---

### Tread carefully

In some organizations, collecting information on project problems can be extraordinarily sensitive; different people may have different agendas for such information. If your PMO is guiding and storing this information, that is for them to manage. If you do not have a PMO managing this for you, confidentiality and professionalism on your part become critical. Remember, the goal of a project evaluation is **not** to target people as the problem. Sure, sometimes people *are* the problem… but people will always have their failings, despite their best efforts. Just as we assume that no pilot is trying to crash the plane, we assume no team member is trying to destroy the project. In general, the goal cannot be to blame people. In general, we want to find process solutions that mitigate the possibility of problems even given the human factor. In short: blame doesn't help, so tread carefully and focus on solutions.

---

## An example: Project Olympus

Consider the following example. Imagine you have been working on a project we will call Project Olympus. During your project, you have documentation that shows orders by your purchasing department colleague Chelone (the Greek god of lateness) are always two to four weeks late. Likewise, they always work from home, and you have trouble getting them to attend meetings in person. But they are always available by e-mail – and you can always find them online, working from home. Several things can happen at this moment:

**1** You make a note of this in your lessons learnt database. You note that when working with purchasing, if they assign Chelone to your efforts, Chelone's orders always seem to arrive two to four weeks behind schedule. Plus, Chelone works best by e-mail. Do not expect Chelone to attend meetings in person.

As a project manager, this may seem like a perfectly reasonable note. You have captured a lesson learnt. You have developed a go-forward strategy for mitigating problems. You move on. If this is where your analysis stops, one can argue that you may have missed the point of the review.

**2** The 'Big Boss' (Zeus), to whom all the departments ultimately report, sees this lesson learnt. Zeus is upset with Chelone's performance, and allows Chelone to stay at home all the time, by terminating Chelone's employment.

That might not be the worst of it...

**3** Imagine that the head of the purchasing department liked having Chelone on their staff, because while Chelone was always a bit optimistic in the delivery dates, they never took sick days, were always available – albeit at home – and had a special relationship with that one vendor living on Changuu Island. You have now made yourself an enemy of the purchasing department, because it was your data that upset the balance of things. By the way, you will need the purchasing department to support you on your next project. How do you think that support will play out, given the preceding?

**4** And, even if you feel you have everything backed up by facts, there could be workplace legal implications as well – because Chelone has now suffered a loss, and Chelone may feel there were other circumstances that your notes do not take into account. For example, the system they use still has to get final approval from accounting, and that process interface was the source of the two-week delays. You didn't know this, and Chelone has now been unfairly opened to ridicule and loss of job.

This is obviously a contrived example, but the point is that, when you're making notes about lessons learnt, there can be real, political, social, organizational and even legal implications to your raw notes. What you think is simply objective data, another person might see as offensive. There may be all types of organizational guidelines, policies and directives regarding such things.

By the way, some organizations do actually use project review information to guide a person's yearly performance evaluation. In this case, typically HR is involved, and they will have their guidelines for how such information is to be recorded, evaluated, reviewed and secured. It all depends on your organization.

I know I've said it already in this chapter, but it's important enough to bear saying again – from our perspective as a project manager, the project review is *not* to be about personal failings. Instead, it should be about looking at the process, and how to make the process work better even in the face of the human factor (which will never be 100 per cent perfect). The real finding from our example above should not be that Chelone is the problem; the real finding is most likely that there is a lead time and lag time involved in working with the purchasing department. It might be that a study needs to look into the source of this lead time and lag time. Until a root cause has been identified, a working solution may be to include a buffer around the estimates from the purchasing department to manage the resulting variances.

The above alternative finding focuses on the *process*, not the person. The purchasing department may still have problems with your finding, because it is not getting to the root cause, which in this case may be the interface to the accounting department. By using this type of approach, you can now engage with them to sort out how they might want you to interact with them more effectively, and how changes to the process might make things run better.

# The accidental, not-so-accidentally successful project manager

The worst thing that can happen to a new project manager is for their project to be an unmitigated success. Stay with me here – of course we want your project to be successful! But if it is an *unmitigated* success, you will likely have no idea what really made that success possible. Then you might be given a bigger project, followed by a bigger project, and eventually a huge project. Finally, the inevitable happens. A problem occurs. At that point, you will not have developed skills for managing through small problems, so you will be completely unequipped for managing this huge problem.

By contrast, the best thing that can happen to a project manager early on is to be challenged by projects that have mild accidents, slight *faux pas*, the awkward oversight issues, kerfuffles that are more amusing than horrible (even though it could have been so much worse), and all the little trials that did not go so well. The skills, insights, checklists (and forms and templates, and the like), methods and tools you develop and refine in managing through these smaller problems become invaluable to the next project, and the next one, and the one after that.

This is not about some motivational cliché. If your first project (or any project along the way) fails too badly, business is not likely to be as forgiving as an inspirational poster might suggest; your career as a project manager may come to an abrupt end. So of course, work your hardest to make this project, and every project, as successful as possible. Always use the guidance of those around you, and seek help and direction from other project managers in your organization, the local PMO, and of course the governance team that you have assembled.

Fortunately, rarely is a project an unmitigated failure or an unmitigated success. In this grey zone between the two extremes, the 'accidents' that happen along the way become your most valuable educational moments. As you develop solutions, it is critical that you capture these moments and build a foundation for a better future. This is why project evaluations can become the most important part of a project: they build the foundation that will make you a successful project manager. Through the review process, project-by-project improvements in skills, processes, methods and tools occur. Your projects eventually become as boringly successful as the average commercial flight.

## Summary points

- When problems are identified, improvement comes not from assigning blame, but from identifying what can be done to keep the problem from developing again in the future.

- Typical project evaluation goals include:
  - What did not go so well and why?
  - What worked well on this project that could be leveraged in other projects?
  - What was the track record of vendors, organizations, departments and people?
  - What alternative measures could be taken to mitigate problems?
  - How might one improve current forms, checklists, templates, standards, tools or procedures?
  - Could organizational changes and recommendations help?

- Work with your PMO to run the post-project evaluation. If you do not have a PMO, work with your governance team to establish organizationally appropriate guidelines.

- Confidentiality and professionalism on your part are critical. Keep raw data confidential.

- Individual people may have been responsible for the initiating event of a problem, but rarely are they the systemic problem.

- Stay focused on systemic things that can be improved. Specifically, consider:

- the chain of events that allowed an issue to become a problem;
- the checklists (flows, forms, templates, and the like);
- processes used;
- equipment and tools;
- methods of communication;
- definitions of team roles and responsibilities;
- skills and training;
- organizational reinforcements;
- compensating methods, and so on.

## Reference

Gawande, A (2011) *The Checklist Manifesto: How to get things right*, Profile Books, London

'Paul J Fielding has created an excellent and thorough overview of the art and science of project management. The book is filled with fun stories and relevant examples. The summary at the end of each chapter will make this *the* must-have reference guide from the C-Suite to the those studying for their PMP exam.'
**Tom Deierlein, CEO, ThunderCat Technology**

'Paul J Fielding manages to demystify the technical aspects of project management by making the concepts practical and easy to understand. He brings project management to life with real stories and examples that will help any reader visualize what needs to be done and provides tips on how to avoid problems.

He also offers valuable insights on when to follow an agile approach and when the old-fashioned waterfall model remains the best option. The reader will find here a book which shows that running a project or programme is about leading – not filling in paperwork about progress made and the like.

When I am working with senior executives on turning around difficult situations, I keep asking the same question: What is the story? This is exactly what this book is about.'
**Eric Lefebvre, author and insurance senior executive**

'*How to Manage Projects* by Paul J Fielding is the definitive guide to understanding the elements and nuances of successful project management. The attention to detail as well as the wealth of in-depth research and advice the book offers is almost too good to be true.'
**Ira Yoffe, Creative Director, Realogy**

'Paul J Fielding gets to the heart of what drives successful outcomes in project management – the foundational principles that inform scope definition, guide governance, align teams, leverage best practices, advise execution methodology and drive continuous improvement from one project to the next. His book shows how you can elevate your practice and leadership through the deeper understanding that successful projects demand a values-driven conflux of varied processes, skills and judgment.'
**Beverley Sutherland, Digital Executive (IBM, HBO, AOL, Citi, A&E Television, Siegel+Gale)**

'Great read for project management professionals, consultants and even entrepreneurs. I particularly enjoyed the examples that bring theoretical project management concepts to life. Paul J Fielding's book is an excellent reference guide on the art and science of project management.'
**Martin Vonderheiden, Instructor, Stanford Continuing Studies, Director, Startup Leadership Program**

'Project management is a critical skill required for success across industry and function, and yet so many get it wrong. This book lays out the principles and techniques needed to drive projects for PMPs and beginners alike. Reading Paul J Fielding's book will arm you and your organization for operational excellence!'
**Jonathan Bartlett, VP Product, Contently**

CPSIA information can be obtained
at www.ICGtesting.com
Printed in the USA
BVHW060945030719
552587BV00019B/90/P

9 780749 488697